2011
NHL DRAFT
GUIDE

ISBN-13: 978-0986538636 (The Hockey Press)

ISBN-10: 0986538639

Printed in the United States of America

HP Story

In 2004 I was coaching Wayne Simmonds in AAA hockey. It was crystal clear to me that Wayne had elite talent. I wondered how a player so talented could go under the radar and be completely missed by the hockey world for so long. It was midway through that season that I had the idea, and HockeyProspect.com was born.

It's over 6 years later and Wayne has gone on to be a very good NHL player. I have been lucky enough to move along in the coaching ranks and have coached other players who are now in the NHL and others who may be there soon.

HockeyProspect.com has had another great year. Our website traffic continues to grow as do our friendships in the hockey world.

I'm proud of the people involved with HockeyProspect.com. They are huge fans of the game and are passionate about their crafts, whether it be scouting or writing. We have some truly talented scouts and equally talented writers and interviewers. The summer of 2011 will be spent updating our website again as we prepare for the 2011/2012 season.

Mark Edwards
Founder
HockeyProspect.com

Acknowledgements

This book would not have been possible without the efforts and long hours put in by our team of both scouts and writers. I want to make special mention of Ryan Yessie who worked extra hard in his first season with us. All of our team members are dedicated and love the sport.

I also want to thank Paul Krotz of the CHL. He is a busy man who has always makes time for us at HockeyProspect.com

To all the photographers who show off their talents in the photos we use both in this draft guide and on our website. Thanks for making the game come alive through your photos.

Thanks to Swiss National coach Sean Simpson, who is spending more time scouting himself these days. I'm looking forward to having more hockey conversation with him this summer.

Finally, I'd like to make a special mention of the late E.J Maguire of NHL Central Scouting. E.J was always willing to help whenever I contacted him. I saw E.J at an OHL game not long before his passing. He was as classy that day as always. The hockey world and many others will miss him.

Thanks,

Mark

Contents

1

SCOUTING REPORTS

Ryan Nugent-Hopkins

Center – Red Deer Rebels (WHL)
Born Apr 12 1993 - Burnaby, BC
Height 6.00 - Weight 163 - Shoots L

HOCKEYPROSPECT.COM

ROUND ONE #1

Games	Goals	Assists	Points	PIMS	+/-
69	31	75	106	51	29

Ryan Nugent-Hopkins was drafted 1st overall in the 2008 WHL Bantam Draft from his hometown program the Burnaby Winter Club Bruins. The Burnaby B.C. Native immediately heard comparisons to former NHL star Joe Sakic. However the comparisons go beyond their hometown, as Nugent-Hopkins showed his excellent hands, and ability to make high difficulty passes right from day one. Nugent-Hopkins gave the WHL a brief view of his talents putting up 6 points in 5 games as an underage player. In his first full season he scored 24 goals, and put up 65 points and won the WHL Rookie of the year.

RNH's skills are highlighted by his remarkable passing abilities, amazing vision and high hockey IQ . He is a prospect with the elite ability to set up his line mates on a regular basis with high difficulty passing and make it look so easy. Although not with the goal scoring acumen of Stamkos, RNH's offensive creativity is at a very high level. He is able to do this because of his elite vision and ability to see plays before they happen. "He sees everything on the ice, all at once." says a highly regarded WHL shutdown defenseman, which may sum up his offensive abilities in one sentence. In addition to his passing abilities, goal scoring is an under-rated part of his game. Nugent-Hopkins has the ability to receive or control the puck and release it in such a quick motion, that it can be very deceptive, and difficult for goaltenders to handle.

RNH is also an excellent skater. Not just because of his speed, but because he is extremely elusive, and can stop and start on a dime. Nugent-Hopkins also has outstanding positioning. If you follow him on the ice for a few games you really begin to appreciate his high end talent and feel for the game. RNH isn't without his areas of improvements, and would benefit from adding some muscle to his frame. In addition RNH could improve his defensive game. Nugent-Hopkins generally doesn't go into the dirty areas and fight for the puck, partially due to lack of strength. Although there are prospects like Landeskog, who are more NHL ready, we feel Nugent-Hopkins ultimately has the highest potential of any eligible player in the 2011 NHL Entry Draft.

Adam Larsson

Defense– Skelleftea HC (SWE)
Born Nov 12 1992
Height 6.02 - Weight 209 - Shoots R

ROUND ONE #2

Games	Goals	Assists	Points	PIMS	+/-
37	1	8	9	41	NA

Defenseman Adam Larsson has one thing that cannot be taught: size. At 6-foot-3 and 220 pounds, the 18-year-old blueliner has an NHL-ready body. Couple that frame with top-flight skills and you have a dynamic prospect. He may even be ahead of fellow Swede Victor Hedman in terms of development at the same age. His multiple years of experience in the Swedish Elite League will be very attractive to NHL teams with top-five picks, a spot Larsson is sure to be selected.

Smooth may be the most appropriate term when describing Larsson's game. He has a very powerful skating stride and great agility. Larsson's acceleration is also very impressive along with his exceptional backward skating and lateral movement, traits that are key to a mobile defenseman. Larsson's hands are terrific for a blueliner, let alone someone of his size. He looks extremely comfortable firing a hard first pass out of the defensive zone or lugging the puck up the ice himself. He has a hard, heavy shot that is accurate from the point. Larsson certainly has the ability to lead a power play at the NHL level. His poise and physical play will allow him to take the ice in all situations.

Larsson will undoubtedly get even more physically imposing in the coming years. Using his size to his advantage more frequently will come with adjusting to the North American game and a smaller rink. He may be the most NHL-ready player in this draft because of his size and experience at the professional level. His poise and play recognition make him one of the safer picks this year as well. His steady play at the World Junior Championships only reiterated to scouts how patient Larsson is for such a young player. For a team looking at a prospect to step in immediately and make a contribution, Larsson will be difficult to pass up.

Jonathan Huberdeau

Center – Saint John Sea Dogs   (QMJHL)
Born Jun 4 1993 - St-Jerome, PQ
Height 6.01 - Weight 170 - Shoots L

HOCKEYPROSPECT.COM

ROUND ONE #3

Games	Goals	Assists	Points	PIMS	+/-
67	43	62	105	88	+59

Jonathan Huberdeau is probably the best 2-way forward available for the draft. He played on the first penalty killing unit at 16 years of age with a championship caliber team in Saint John which shows the trust the coaching had in him at a young age.

Jonathan Huberdeau is a magnificent puck handler and he uses those skills to escape active sticks from opposing players. He is shifty and strong on his skates. He always has his head up and can find an open man from just about anywhere in the offensive zone. He is a fantastic playmaker but don't underestimate his scoring skills. He has a good shot that he releases at anytime from anywhere on the ice. He could shoot even more than he does with the space he is able to create for himself. He creates a lot of turnovers using his great anticipation skills. He doesn't shy away from physicality and can keep the puck with pressure on him, but he doesn't initiate physicality too often. He produces a lot offensively in 5-on-5 situations because he can adapt to any situation. If he has to cycle the puck to create an opportunity he will do it. Sometimes when a fancy game doesn't work, you have to come back to a more basic game and that's something he is able to recognize. Huberdeau has a fantastic work ethic. It rivals not only anyone is his draft class but in the entire CHL.

When Huberdeau improves his explosiveness and his speed a little bit, he will be a scary package. We have no doubt that Huberdeau will become an impact 2-way forward at the NHL level. With more pounds added on to that frame and more strength, he will only get better.

 Jonathan should impress in the interviews at the combine. We came away very impressed after our two interviews with him this season. He is a mature and very likeable young man. He understands that hockey is played in 3 zones and that a commitment is needed in all three zones to become a complete player. When you add on his scoring and playmaking talents, the words 'elite player' comes to mind.

Mika Zibanejad

Center – Djurgarden (SWE)
Born April 18 1993 - Huddinge, SWE
Height 6.02 - Weight 192 - Shoots R

Games	Goals	Assists	Points	PIMS	+/-
26	5	4	9	2	NA

Mika Zibanejad might be the most interesting player in the 2011 draft. We saw him first when he put on a show at the 2010 World Under-17 Hockey Challenge in Timmins. The 6'1" 190 pounder led Sweden with 5 goals and 9 points in six games. He was already producing back in Sweden but when players like Zibanejad shine in North America their draft stock always makes a big jump up the rankings.

Mika is a big hard working two-way forward who has as quick a release as we have seen in a long while for a kid at his stage of development. The puck explodes off his stick. His skating is not pretty but he is very quick, a bit ugly but effective might be a way to describe his skating. He uses slightly short choppy strides to dance all over the ice but he does it with pretty good speed and he gets after it. This kid looks like the energizer bunny at times. He is not afraid to go to the dirty areas and he forechecks like nobody's business. Mika sees the ice very well and is as adept at playmaking as he is to scoring with his fantastic shot and soft hands. In short, this kid is just a blast to watch. He seems to be having as much fun as the fans who are watching him. He is not shy about smiling.

Mika is a converted winger and now plays center on the 3rd line for Djurgarden in Sweden. He is a reliable player who can be used in all situations. He is proud of his overall game and when we chatted with him it really came through. This is a player who loves to compete every shift and be counted on in close games and clutch situations. He is relied on for penalty kill and he gets some powerplay minutes. When we asked Mika what was the weakest part of his game he told us, "I want to work on my skating. I need to become more explosive and work on my acceleration."

He has great vision on the ice, is hard working and he has an outstanding shot with a quick release to go along with a 6'2" 190 pound frame. Just imagine how good he might be if he makes progress on the acceleration and explosiveness he spoke about.

Sean Couturier

Center – Drummondville (QMJHL)
Born Dec 7 1992 - Bathurst, NB
Height 6.03 - Weight 198 - Shoots L

ROUND ONE #5

Games	Goals	Assists	Points	PIMS	+/-
58	36	60	96	36	+55

There has been quite a buzz around the young Drummondville Voltigeurs center over the last couple of years and he has managed to keep a level head and play through it all. Couturier exploded on to the scene during his teams Memorial Cup run. For an encore he led the QMJHL in scoring the next season.

Couturier is a big, strong kid. He has improved his skating in the last few years but it has a ways to go. His small area starts and stops were exposed a bit during testing in Toronto at the Top Prospects Game. We take testing with a grain of salt, but he was one player that really stood out during testing. Sean showed sluggish starts from a standstill and heavy feet. Having said that, Ryan O'Reilly had skating issues as well and made the NHL right away as a 2nd rounder.

Sean's speed is fine once he gets rolling and he can create so much by using his puck protection skills. Couturier also has good hands and he has a heavy wrist shot. He wins most of the faceoffs he takes. He has the tools to be a really good player, but what separates him from the others is his hockey I.Q. His hockey smarts in the offensive zone and in the defensive zone make him a really solid all-around player. The Voltigeurs have given him almost 30 minutes of icetime per game since the beginning of the season. He wins most of his battles along the boards and he makes quick decisions with the puck without causing turnovers. His execution is a notch a higher than most players in major junior.

Sean holds his spot in our top 5 based on his overall play. He has a high hockey IQ and with his size, scoring ability and competitive nature, it makes him a natural fit to succeed at the NHL level. He will be able to play in all situations in the NHL which makes him a player who can play big minutes. With his intelligence we can see him making the required tweaks to his game pretty quicky and he should make an impact in the NHL early in his career. We project him as a future number one Center in the NHL.

Gabriel Landeskog

Right Wing– Kitchener Rangers (OHL)
Born Nov 23 1992 - Stockholm, SWE
Height 6.01 - Weight 207 - Shoots L

Games	Goals	Assists	Points	PIMS	+/-
53	36	30	66	61	+27

Gabriel Landeskog made an immediate impact in Kitchener, even though many forget he was actually drafted by the Plymouth Whalers 3rd overall in the 2009 CHL Import Draft. He was traded about a month after the draft to Kitchener. Despite being caught behind some strong talent up front in Kitchener in his rookie season, Landeskog made an impact scoring in 3 of his first 5 games, and hasn't slowed down since. Landeskog was named Kitchener Rangers captain; as a 17 year old import player. This is unheard of in the CHL, but is a tribute to his great leadership which he is able to project with both his words, and his play.

Landeskog plays a Power Forward's game, throwing big hits, and finishing his checks whenever possible. He is a tireless worker along the boards. Offensively, Gabriel has a great shot, very good hands, and is able to beat opposing players 1 on 1. He is also is an excellent puck protector and showed us the ability to go end to end and work around players using his body very effectively. Landeskog not only can shoot the puck, but he makes great plays with the puck. He makes some high difficulty plays, but seems very aware of his surroundings and the plays developing around him, always checking before making a high risk play. Making mistakes with the puck is a few and far between occurrence for Gabriel. His awareness and mobility is one of the things that separates Landeskog from other players of similar size. He reads the play as it's developing, and does the little things like covering the point for a pinching defenseman. On his own side of the red line, Landeskog works just as hard, particularly in the corners, and takes pride in his ability to battle below his own goal line, and helping the defense take the puck out of the zone.

Gabriel really seems to love playing at home in front of the loud crowd in Kitchener, however, Ranger fans may not see much more of Gabriel. We consider Landeskog to be the most NHL ready prospect in this year's draft, we expect him to stick with whoever selects him for the 2011-2012 NHL Season.

Ryan Murphy

Defense – Kitchener Rangers (OHL)
Born Mar 31 1993 - Aurora, ONT
Height 5.11 - Weight 165 - Shoots R

Games	Goals	Assists	Points	PIMS	+/-
63	26	53	79	36	+22

Ryan Murphy was selected 3rd overall in the 2009 OHL Priority Selection by the Kitchener Rangers; the first defenseman selected in the draft. Ryan played for a powerhouse York-Simcoe Express team which also produced 1st Overall pick Daniel Catenacci, Barclay Goodrow, and Brandon Francisco in the same year. Murphy didn't take long to settle in, improving at a rapid rate, finishing the year with 39 points in 62 games. Ryan opened the season as Kitchener's #1 defenseman, and has maintained that role with a few brief stints atop the leagues scoring race. Murphy eventually was a final cut for the Canadian roster in the WJC.

Ryan Murphy has the ability to change a game at the CHL level. He impacts a game with his great skating ability. Murphy is a very mobile defenseman. He has a top gear he can activate that makes him one of the fastest skaters in the league. Murphy is an excellent puck mover, and runs the power play on most opportunities. He also has a massive point shot, evidence of this is in his goal totals. Murphy's conditioning is excellent. He can spend over 25-30 minutes per game and still maintains intelligent decision making and composure. Murphy is starting to make better choices deciding when to jump into the rush. When he does, he has no fear of driving to the net. Murphy will need to overcome his size. He does however seem to handle physical punishment well, and has shown a willingness to throw hits himself. Murphy's play in his own zone is respectable, and improving on a steady basis. He manages to defend well considering his size by using a very active stick and using solid positional play. However, Ryan loses a lot of battles out front of his own net.

Although a top prospect, Ryan Murphy will likely need a few more years before becoming an NHL regular. He'll need to get physically stronger to handle the physicality of the NHL, and get better at handling forwards much bigger than he is. Murphy will probably create a new position in the NHL. He will be a first unit PP defenseman, who will be challenged to crack a top three defense spot on his team. We would be happy to have him on our team.

Nathan Beaulieu

Defense– Saint John Sea Dogs (QMJHL)
Born Dec 5 1992 - Strathroy, ONT
Height 6.01 - Weight 190 - Shoots L

Games	Goals	Assists	Points	PIMS	+/-
65	12	33	45	52	+44

On a very solid young and talented team in St-John, Beaulieu has proven that he is the real deal. Beaulieu has been given powerplay time this season and his point production has been very impressive.

Nathan is a late 1992 birthdate. He was listed at 6'1", 190 pounds in Toronto for the prospects event and is a good skater. When he rushes the puck he is very shifty and difficult to stop. His head is up and he sees the ice very well. He makes good decisions off the rush. Nathan does a good job joining the rush as well. He is good at jumping into the play and becoming an option and uses his hockey smarts to find a quiet spot and surprise the opposing team in their own zone.

He's always moving his feet when he's on the ice. On the powerplay it's really tough to adjust to him. He's got good puck skills and either finds seams or creates them. He can take unnecessary risks once in a while but these are becoming fewer and far between of late. Nathan is one of the reasons the Sea Dogs have scored so many goals in the 2010-2011 season. HP's Director of Scouting, Mark Edwards, had this to say about Beaulieu, "He really stood out the first time I saw him live last summer. I remember thinking that he should be a lock for the top 10 overall. His head was always up and he knew when to dish the puck or when he could go with it. I wondered if he was always that good. He can be pretty physical at times too, which no team will complain about."

Beaulieu's biggest problems early on this season were caused by a lack of consistency. Sometimes he tried to do too much rather than just simplify his game. He got back on track quickly using the boards, making short passes and just getting pucks to the net rather than forcing an ill-advised pass. His shot is good and accurate. An HP favorite who we just don't see escaping the top 10 picks.

Beaulieu is a skilled, intelligent, big defenseman with vision that just needs a little more seasoning. Nathan has a chance to be a first pairing NHL defenseman barring a complete collapse in his game. This kid is a gamer and it was an easy decision placing him in our top 10. We feel that Nathan is a lock to play in the NHL. He is a very safe draft pick.

Ryan Strome

Center – Niagara Ice Dogs (OHL)
Born Jul 11 1993 - Mississauga, ONT
Height 6.00 - Weight 173 - Shoots R

HOCKEYPROSPECT.COM

ROUND ONE #9

Games	Goals	Assists	Points	PIMS	+/-
65	33	73	106	82	+28

Ryan was selected 8th overall by the Barrie Colts in the 2009 OHL Priority Selection out of the Toronto Marlboros program. He joined fellow prospects Lucas Lessio, Brett Ritchie, and Stuart Percy as first round graduates of the Marlboros program. Strome had a quiet but strong start to his career in Barrie. Despite seeing limited minutes, it became very clear that it would be only a matter of time before Strome got the ice time to show his true talent. Strome was a big piece, in the blockbuster deal that involved Alex Pietrangelo going to Barrie, which saw Strome finish his rookie season for the up and coming Niagara Ice Dogs team.

Strome started this season out with a bang, putting up 2 goals in his first game and 26 points in his first 15 games. Strome also accomplished a very interesting feat in the playoffs against the Oshawa Generals, scoring in every single game of that series.

Strome has a ton of offensive upside and is without a doubt one of the most dynamic players in this year's draft. Strome has exceptional puck handling abilities, and when given any space to work, he can put together highlight reel plays. HP founder, Mark Edwards had this to say about Strome. "I remember telling one of our scouts last summer that Strome was very talented but played too much on the perimeter in Minor Midget. It didn't surprise me when he started going into dirty areas that his whole game changed. Ryan started to become a pretty complete player in all 3 zones. I knew how skilled and shifty with the puck he was, but it was when he became willing to pay the price to win pucks all over the ice that he turned the corner for me."

Strome has quick feet and is one of the most dangerous offensive players in this draft. His faceoffs could use work. This was never more evident than in a recent playoff series going up against Boone Jenner. He struggled versus the bigger Jenner and was schooled a bit. The faceoffs are not a huge concern though - he will improve as he gets stronger. Strome has a high hockey IQ and has made players around him better. He has dazzled with both scoring and passing skills this season. A few Dogs should probably put Ryan on their Christmas card list next season. Watch for Strome to go in the top 10 picks in June.

Mark McNeill

Center – Prince Albert Raiders (WHL)
Born Feb 22 1993 - Edmonton, ALTA
Height 6.02 - Weight 201 - Shoots R

Games	Goals	Assists	Points	PIMS	+/-
70	32	49	81	53	-4

Mark McNeill was selected 5th overall in the 2008 WHL Bantam Draft. He joined the Prince Albert Raiders full-time for the 2009-2010 season, and although he received a bit of a limited role at times, and had a few struggles, his potential started to show through at times. However this season, when given a ton of responsibility to help lead the Raiders team, he not only answered the call, but excelled on a consistent basis.

McNeill is first noticeable for his size. He has NHL ready size, and uses it very effectively, as he can throw some devastating hits, will finish his checks whenever possible, and has quite the mean streak on him. What makes this so impressive is, despite the size and physicality, McNeill is an excellent skater. His size and skating ability combined gives him excellent puck control, and he has shown to be capable of scoring highlight reel goals.

What impresses us so much about McNeill, and raises his stock on our rankings is his ability to not only use his skillset to create offense for himself, but also for all 4 of his teammates on the ice. He can be deceptive, due to having a solid release on his shot, but also the ability to thread the needle to teammates. His positioning in the offensive zone is excellent, and he has shown very well in the face-off circle. The biggest concern about McNeill is he shows very little urgency getting back into defensive positioning, and has not done great in his own zone. This must be improved before he makes the next step.

HP's Ryan Yessie says, "McNeill has been a personal favorite of mine all year. He does everything on the offensive side of the red line so well, and makes everyone around him better. It was hard to believe how long he flew under the radar. He has such a dangerous combination of size speed, skill, and hockey sense. He's a threat every time he's in the offensive zone. I really wouldn't be shocked if he made the jump to the NHL as soon as next year, depending on who selects him."

Ty Rattie

Right Wing– Portland (WHL)
Born Feb 5 1993 - Airdrie, ALTA
Height 5.11 - Weight 163 - Shoots R

Games	Goals	Assists	Points	PIMS	+/-
67	28	51	79	55	+20

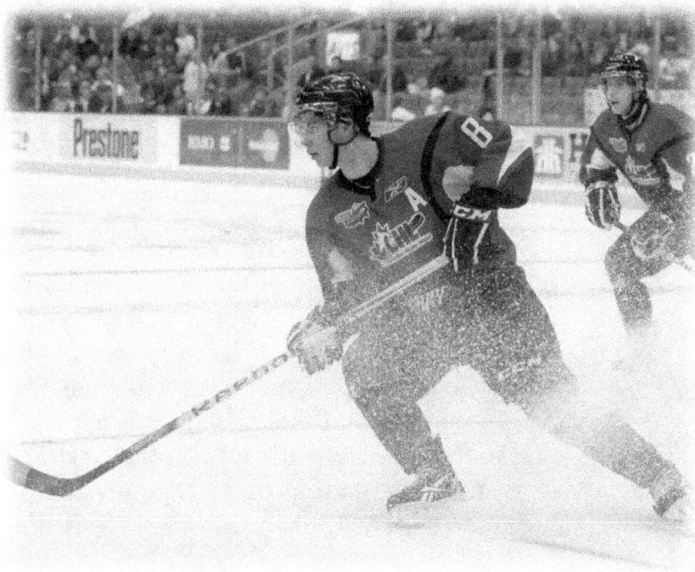

Ty Rattie was selected 2nd overall in the 2008 WHL Bantam Draft only behind potential 1st overall pick in the 2011 NHL Entry Draft Ryan Nugent-Hopkins. Rattie then played Midget AAA as a 15 year old, before joining Portland. Last season Rattie started to show off why he was hyped, despite being behind highly touted Ryan Johansen, Nino Niederreiter, and Bradley Ross for the 2010 NHL Draft, Rattie quietly showed his potential. This season Ty has put up good numbers for a second year player, and even better numbers in the playoffs.

Ty Rattie's biggest standout skill has to be his hands. He is extremely quick and handles the puck expectionally well. Rattie is easily one of the most dangerous players in the draft if he gets the puck in the offensive zone, and makes opponents pay when they give him any time or space. Ty is extremely elusive and more often than not will win a 1 on 1 battle whether it be coming off the boards or flying down on a rush. He has outstanding vision, and has great understanding on the concept between when to shoot and when to pass. He is dangerous in both scenarios due to his ability to complete high difficulty passes, but also having a quick release on his shot. Because of this, and his great creativity, he is capable of making plays for both himself and his linemates, and keeps the opposition guessing.

Rattie doesn't quite have that explosiveness in his skating that we'd like to see in a top prospect at his level. Regardless, he is very smooth and is good when he gets to top speed. His skating can't be considered a flaw due to those facts. Despite his size, Rattie does respectably well in the corners, and battles hard, even though he doesn't have the size yet. Ultimately, the only areas we'd like to see Ty improve in his explosiveness in his skating, as well as upper body strength. He can hit the weight room to improve both and if the team who selects him pushes a good strength conditioning

Boone Jenner

Center – Oshawa Generals (OHL)
Born Jun 15 1993 - Dorchester, ONT
Height 6.01 - Weight 204 - Shoots L

ROUND ONE #12

Games	Goals	Assists	Points	PIMS	+/-
63	25	41	66	57	+10

Jenner was the 4th overall pick in the 2009 OHL Draft and did not take long to impress the hometown Oshawa fans in his first season in the OHL. Jenner finished second to Matt Puempel in rookie scoring, with 19 goals and 49 points.

The 6-foot-1, 204 pound center is a hockey player in every sense of the word. Jenner is a player that any coach worth his salt would want on his team. Much like we told anyone who would listen a couple years ago when we spoke about Ryan O'Reilly, Jenner is a kid who will play in the NHL. Jenner is a physical player who can be flat out nasty at times and just be a pain to play against.

Jenner is also very skilled and can beat you with his offensive talent. He can shoot, handle the puck in traffic and is a dominant force along the walls. You don't need to interview Boone to figure out that this kid is a fierce competitor. Use any phrase you want; 'he's a warrior', a 'workhorse' or 'a guy you want to go to war with'. Whatever you choose describes why you want him on your side.

To put it simply, Boone is an all-around hockey player. He is a dynamite faceoff guy who can just as easily play the powerplay as play on the penalty kill. You don't need to watch the Generals too often to see that he is a leader on the team. He can dominate periods let alone shifts. We love his compete level and that motor that runs non-stop.

Finally this brings us to the biggest reason we have raised Jenner's draft ranking this year. Boone has come miles in the skating department this season. In a game at the NHL research camp back in August we took notes about his skating deficiencies. Flash forward to a recent playoff game in which we saw him beat a defenseman wide with speed after lugging the puck end to end on a powerplay breakout. It would be fun to watch Boone at his first NHL camp. He will play in the NHL for whoever drafts him....who knows, maybe even next fall.

Sven Bärtschi

Left Wing– Portland (WHL)
Born Oct 5 1992 - Langenthal, SUI
Height 5.10 - Weight 181 - Shoots L

Games	Goals	Assists	Points	PIMS	+/-
66	34	51	85	84	+23

Bartschi is a highly talented Swiss born winger playing his first season in the Western Hockey League. Bartschi just completed a very strong season playing on a line with Ty Rattie, another 2011 draft prospect.

HP's Mark Edwards had this to say about Bartschi. "My first impression was that he was highly skilled. His shot is deadly accurate and he has a quick release. He is a dangerous forward. I think Sven summed himself up pretty nicely when I spoke to him at the World Jr's in Buffalo. In short, he said that he is the scorer while Ty (Rattie) is more of a playmaker. Bartschi was not overly impressive in Buffalo because he just refused to go into any dirty areas. With that said, I thought he was a fantastic kid with a great sense of humor. Another scout and I walked away from chatting with him both saying how impressed we were with his personal skills. I have liked his game more since that time. I have watched Portland quite a few times on tape since Buffalo and he has been much better than my first impression. One of our Western scouts, Jason Hills, is very high on him."

Bartschi has shown that he can score. He has speed, smarts, a great shot with a quick release, and very soft hands. What remains to be seen is Bartschi's willingness to compete for pucks on a regular basis. He is not a big kid, so we are not expecting him to lead his team in PIM's or body checks. We just want him to 'get after it' a little bit more.

In the end, Bartschi might be a boom or bust type player. He is still young and will probably develop more of a desire to mix it up a bit as he gets older. He is not a strong player, so it goes without saying that he is going to need to focus on building up some bulk and core strength to help prepare himself to play against men in the NHL.

Scott Mayfield

Defense – Youngstown USHL)
Born Oct 14 1992 - St. Louis, MO
Height 6.04 - Weight 197- Shoots R

Games	Goals	Assists	Points	PIMS	+/-
52	7	9	16	159	-18

Playing with a physical edge is something that many young defensemen struggle with. Not Scott Mayfield. The Youngstown Phantoms' blueliner has a nasty streak and the size to go with it. At 6-foot-4 and 200 pounds, Mayfield has a slender frame but has added muscle the past few years. With a tougher training regimen in the future, his body will mature quickly. Mayfield has a nice skill set to go along with his improving physique. He models his game after Chris Pronger and if he reaches that level of play, one NHL team is going to land a gem come June.

HP has been very high on Mayfield for quite a while. He is an extremely complete player. Despite his size, Mayfield is an excellent skater. He has a long stride and good quickness. His puck skills are also terrific. Mayfield is able to corral the puck and make quick passes. His hockey sense allows him to make the right play more often than not. His play without the puck is exceptional to go along with good gap control and positioning. Mayfield's offensive skills are vastly underrated. He hasn't posted great numbers in the United States Hockey League, but the skills are there. He has a solid shot and makes accurate tape-to-tape passes.

Mayfield is prone to the odd costly mistake at times, as pressure makes him force the pass into dangerous areas. Gaining more confidence in his abilities will allow Mayfield to feel more relaxed, yet make smarter, quicker plays. He is off to the University of Denver next season where he will hone his skills in a terrific hockey program. Mayfield will not play in the NHL right away, but he could become a top-pair defenseman in the future.

Oscar Klefbom

Defense– Farjestads (SWE)
Born Jul 20 1993, Karlstad, SWE
Height 6.04 - Weight 200 - Shoots L

 ROUND ONE #15

Games	Goals	Assists	Points	PIMS	+/-
23	1	1	2	2	NA

How do we describe this kid? When we talk about Swedish defensemen this year we focus on three of them. Adam Larsson, Jonas Brodin and the subject of this profile, Oscar Klefbom.

Despite the offensive skills that an Adam Larsson possesses, Klefbom probably has the biggest upside when it comes to rush the puck and blasting it from the blueline. Klefbom plays a very aggressive brand of hockey. He is more of a do-er while Brodin and Larsson are much more cerebral players. Both Brodin and Klefbom play for Farjestads in Sweden. Larsson plays for Skelleftea.

One of the more interesting scenarios in this draft will be to see if an NHL team values Oscar's flashy rushes, bigger size and cannon shot, over the more safe Brodin, who understands his position as well as anyone in this draft. Klefbom sports both a hard slap shot and a very hard wrist shot. If this were baseball you might call his wrist shot 'heavy' as baseball folks refer to some pitchers fastballs. Klefbom's wrist shot is hard and accurate. Oscar loves to jump into the rush and he does a decent job of deciding when to do it. He sees the ice well and does a good job of dishing the puck off the rush to a teammate, only to get it back later. It's obvious that he loves to rush the puck. His great skating ability, which sports a pretty good burst of speed, allows him to do it.

Klefbom has his weaknesses. He is not exactly what we would refer to as a shutdown guy. He works hard in his own zone and has a high motor, but he loses his man too often. Sometimes he is just lost on where he needs to be. He struggles at times to think the game quickly enough in his own zone. While he is elite in the offensive end of the ice, he is a work in progress in the other end. Klefbom is a very solid prospect who could surprise many depending on when he gets selected on draft day. Nothing would really shock us. We see him as a first round talent.

Jamie Oleksiak

Defense – Northeastern (NCAA)
Born Dec 21 1992 - Toronto, ONT
Height 6.07 - Weight 244 - Shoots L

Games	Goals	Assists	Points	PIMS	+/-
38	4	9	13	57	+15

Born in Toronto, this huge specimen has been playing south of the border. This year Oleksiak is a freshman with Northeastern and was previously in the USHL with the Chicago Steel. HP founder Mark Edwards on Jamie, "I'm not sure if anyone has progressed as much as this kid has over the last couple of years. I suspect his name will be called quite early in Minnesota. Imagine Hal Gill as an elite skater with great feet and some offensive skills. Jamie still needs some work as far some decisions with the puck are concerned. His skating is amazing for his size but he leaves too big a gap too often for my liking. He shows that he can do it, but his consistency in that area needs to improve. I like the way he is willing to jump into the rush. It's a work in progress but if this part of his game clicks, look out."

Oleksiak is huge. He is listed at 6'7" 244 and was measured by NHL Central scouting so it's legit. It's not often that you get a kid this big that can skate the way Jamie can skate. He has great edges and looks like a giant in the path of forwards trying to beat him one on one. The wingspan is pretty entertaining to watch in action. He uses his stick really well and his reach might span the width of the old Boston Garden. Not only can this kid defend, he is also game to contribute on offense a little bit. He is fun to watch skate the puck because he is not just a strong skater for his size, he is just a great skater. Along with the skating skill, comes some decent hands, Jamie can handle the puck a little bit as well.

It's not too often that a player can progress as quickly as Jamie has progressed. He has improved his decision making all over the ice from (hate to say it) an 'awful' level just two years ago, to 'good' this season. If that area of his game keeps improving he will have high end shutdown ability. The upside he brings as a 6'7" defender who can skate is quite high. Suddenly Jamie has made himself a very tough prospect to pass on. We suspect he will be snatched up before the 15th pick is taken. Not bad for a kid that was off many NHL scout's radars before the season.

Joe Morrow

Defense – Portland (WHL)
Born Dec 9 1992 - Sherwood Park, ALTA
Height 6.00 - Weight 197 - Shoots L

HOCKEYPROSPECT.COM

ROUND ONE #17

Games	Goals	Assists	Points	PIMS	+/-
60	9	40	49	67	+23

Joe Morrow was taken in the 2nd round of the 2007 WHL Bantam draft by the Portland Winterhawks. Morrow only had 42 games played in his first two seasons active in the WHL, but last year started to show what he could do. Morrow is a late 1992 birthdate and has taken full advantage of this. He has really broken out this season, and has got better as the games have become more important. To top it off, Morrow has played extremely well for Portland in the playoffs and has been a key element to their success.

Morrow's skills are highlighted by his great skating ability. Morrow has smooth strides, and wins races on a regular basis. He has shown this skill regularly to commit to offensive plays, knowing he can close in on forwards if the puck is turned over.

Morrow is very calm and composed with the puck and has the ability to rush the puck up the ice, and acquire the offensive zone a high percentage of the time. Morrow also has the defensive awareness to make the safe play out of the zone when pressured, or spending an extended period in his own zone. He doesn't try to force plays at times like these.

Joe has good offensive instincts and he moves the puck very effectively on the powerplay. He has good patience waiting for a play to open up, and has a respectable shot. We would like to see him shoot more often though. What impressed us about Morrow wasn't just his skill, but the amount in which he improved over the course of the season. He got caught out of position a lot earlier in the year, and although this still happens, it's a much more spaced out occurrence. His strength appeared to be an issue along the boards, in the corners, and in front of the net where he would get out muscled. This is another area he needs to continue to improve on, but it doesn't appear to be the glaring weakness it was a while back. Morrow has a lot of potential to become a top 4 defenseman in the NHL.

Duncan Siemens

Defense – Saskatoon Blades (WHL)
Born Sep 7 1993 - Sherwood Park, ALTA
Height 6.02 - Weight 192 - Shoots L

Games	Goals	Assists	Points	PIMS	+/-
72	5	38	43	121	+40

Duncan Siemens was selected 3rd overall by the Saskatoon Blades after being a top bantam player out of Sherwood Park. If he was born 5 days later he would be eligible for the 2012 NHL Entry Draft. Duncan had a solid full season as a 16 year old, and is mature beyond his years. He was awarded with the "A" to start the season, despite being a 17 year old on a team with high expectations. When Stefan Elliot was returned Siemens showed his maturity by offering up the "A" to Elliot, stating Elliot's veteran status as the reason for why he wanted to give it up.

Duncan has really shown off his great two way ability. He has a cannon of a point shot, and is extremely underrated in the offensive end of the ice. We talked to Duncan after the CHL Top Prospects Game. When asked to describe himself he stated that he is a physical player who likes to get under the skin of the opposition, and have them focused on him, rather than the game going on around them. He also stated he doesn't really care to focus on the rankings, and prefers to focus on his game, and let himself be ranked as others see him. Duncan greatly impresses us with his maturity when speaking with him.

Duncan has proven his physical side and has made himself an extremely difficult defenseman to be matched up against. He has thrown some massive hits, and has been equally as devastating in fights, very rarely ending on the wrong side of the result. He still has some work to do in the defensive zone. He can sometimes miss an assignment, or will be in the wrong position. He has improved on this, but Duncan dropped slightly in our rankings due to his positional play being exposed a little bit in the playoffs. Regardless Siemens is a competitive player, and is just simply too talented to rank outside the top 20. Duncan is physically mature and could be just a few adjustments away from playing in the NHL within the next year or two. Duncan shows the leadership of a future captain in both the CHL and NHL levels.

Stuart Percy

Defense – Mississauga Majors (OHL)
Born May 18 1993 - Oakville, ONT
Height 6.01 - Weight 188 - Shoots R

Games	Goals	Assists	Points	PIMS	+/-
64	4	29	33	50	+50

Stuart Percy was drafted by 15th overall in the 2009 OHL Priority Selection by Mississauga out of the Toronto Marlboros organization. Percy had a respectable rookie season where he didn't see a ton of ice, due to playing for a strong Majors team. This season he has taken control of his own destiny, and played his way into logging big minutes and is used as a critical part of the Majors' blue line in all game situations.

Percy is regarded by both scouts and his peers as an extremely intelligent defenseman, who understands the game well. Percy's highlights include his defensive game, where he exhibits excellent positioning, and can control the movement of oncoming forwards within the rules of the game. Percy has also shown very well in 1 on 1 situations, as well as 2 on 1's. Percy maintains an active stick and exceptional positioning in the defensive zone. He also has great understanding in terms of when to pinch in from the point, and when to get back into defensive positioning. On the offensive side of the game, Percy has shown to more commonly pass the puck up the ice, as supposed to attempting to rush it. Percy is used on the power play and has shown he can make good decisions with the puck when he is under pressure.

Despite being a solid defensive defenseman, Percy has shown he has legitimate two-way potential. He has shown to have good offensive instincts. The biggest thing for Percy's development will be to hit the weight room on a regular basis and to get stronger. Percy has been pushed around by bigger, stronger players at times. This means getting knocked around physically and can lead to losing corner battles despite showing the ability to compete. Percy has a good frame, that can handle a muscle gain, and if he can add a better physical element to his game, Percy could, like in the OHL Priority Selection, turn out to be a huge steal for the team who decides to pick him up. We are very confident in Percy's abilities and how they will translate to the NHL. We love his hockey IQ and project him as a future top 4 NHL defenseman.

Jonas Brodin

Defense– Färjestad (SWE)
Born July 12 1993 - Karlstad, SWE
Height 6.01 - Weight 169 - Shoots L

Games	Goals	Assists	Points	PIMS	+/-
42	0	4	4	12	NA

Like top prospect Adam Larsson, Swedish defenseman Jonas Brodin brings professional experience to the table. He played most of this season for Farjestad in the Swedish Elite League. He saw limited time at Sweden's highest level last season, and he played well enough to get the nod this year. The 6-foot-1, 170-pound blueliner has great hockey sense. He is calm with the puck, and pressure does not seem to faze him. That calm demeanor and poise is one of the most important parts of making it as a defenseman in the NHL.

Couple his unflappable style with terrific mobility and it is easy to see why we like him. Brodin has quick feet and pivots well. His lateral movement is superb. He is solid in all areas of the ice and anticipates the play very well. As puck-moving defenseman are becoming so coveted in today's NHL, Brodin's ability to fire a tape-to-tape first pass will bode well for his hockey future. With his skating ability, he is also able to bring the puck up the ice himself. His offensive skills are solid as well. He has a good, accurate shot, but he has not put up great numbers. Despite his lack of offensive production, Brodin is capable of playing in all situations.

Brodin will likely spend another season or two in Sweden. Bulking up will be essential to his future as an NHL player. He really bangs guys around and wins a lot of battles now based on superior effort alone. He will need both more bulk and his tenacious attitude to do that in the NHL. Brodin has all the tools, but he needs to build a solid frame to take the punishment of a defenseman at the highest level. His experience, mobility and all-around safe play will be very attractive to NHL teams.

Dougie Hamilton

Defense – Niagara Ice Dogs (OHL)
Born Jun 17 1993 - Toronto, ONT
Height 6.05 - Weight 188 - Shoots R

ROUND ONE #21

Games	Goals	Assists	Points	PIMS	+/-
67	12	46	58	77	+35

If there is one player in this draft where we might stray from other's draft board rankings a bit, it would probably be with Hamilton. While some have Hamilton ranked as high as fifth in their overall rankings, we have Hamilton down our board a little bit in the first round.

Dougie was drafted in the second round by the Ice Dogs. Hamilton has been slotted as a high pick for the June draft and with his size and skating ability it's easy to see why he gets so much attention. He is a talented defenseman who has posted big numbers this year on a good Niagara squad. Where we see things a bit differently is in the physical play department and some decision making. We are not crazy about is his lack of consistent physical play or 'push back' and some of his decision making with and without the puck.

Hamilton has good skating ability wrapped up in a huge 6'5" frame. He has a long reach and does a pretty good job of using his stick to poke check and take away lanes. He uses his feet pretty well on the powerplay to get himself to the middle of the ice. He has really improved on reading plays and jumping backdoor or even into the slot to pot some goals. His shot needs to be more accurate. He misses the net or shoots into shin pads too often. Another area where Dougie needs to get more consistent is decision making in the offensive zone. He makes some high risk pinches forcing his partner to play 2 on 1's going the other way too often.

Hamilton can be too easy to play against at times. We think he needs to start playing more to his size more often. While he shows flashes of physical play, it comes in spurts. The raw tools are clearly there but comparisons we heard to players like Pietrangelo are not fair to him. Dougie does not have the offensive skills, or puck rushing ability that Pietrangelo had at the same age. Hamilton plays a more simple, safe game and is not nearly as slick as Pietrangelo was with the puck. It sounds like we are down on him, but we are not. We are simply explaining why we don't have him ranked in the top 5. Hamilton should have a nice NHL career ahead of him

Joel Armia

Right Wing – Ässät (SM- Liiga)
Born May 31 1993 - Pori, Finland
Height 6.03 - Weight 191 - Shoots R

Games	Goals	Assists	Points	PIMS	+/-
48	18	11	29	24	NA

Like many European players, winger Joel Armia has superb offensive skills. "The Finnish Ace," as he is known in Finland, has posted 17 goals and 25 points in 38 games for Assat in his first season in Finland's top professional league, SM-liiga. But in six games at the 2011 IIHF U20 World Junior Championship in Buffalo, N.Y., Armia registered just one point. Finland lost to Russia in the semifinal round.

At 6-foot-3, Armia has great size and wins many physical battles. Armia will still need to fill out his large frame to be a physical force at the NHL level. He has many offensive tools at this stage in his career. With his size, Armia protects the puck well down low. He isn't afraid to go into the hard areas to score, something that will undoubtedly help him transition to the tighter-checking North American game. His hockey sense is above average, and he makes nifty plays around the net while showing the flare that many European players possess. Armia has a quick release and a very accurate and heavy shot. He has great hands and although he is probably a better scorer, he is adept as a playmaker as well. Armia also skates very well for a big player. While his first few steps could certainly improve, he has a good, long stride once he gets going. His deficiencies come in the defensive zone. Armia will need to make a stronger commitment to becoming a two-way player in order to succeed in the NHL. He is also prone to taking a shift off now and then, while merely gliding around the ice.

Armia certainly has the skills to be a top-six NHL forward. Gaining strength will be critical to his continued physical development. That will come with a serious off-ice commitment and a professional workout routine.

Matt Puempel

Left Wing – Peterborough Petes (OHL)
Born Jan 24 1993 - Essex, ONT
Height 6.00 - Weight 196 - Shoots L

HOCKEYPROSPECT.COM

ROUND ONE #23

Games	Goals	Assists	Points	PIMS	+/-
55	34	35	69	49	-33

Matthew Puempel emerged from the Sun County Panthers program as a top prospect, highlighted by 88 goals in 76 Games. The Petes selected him 4th overall in the 2009 OHL Priority Selection, and he put up 33 goals in his rookie season. Matt Puempel went on to be the OHL Rookie Scoring leader. In fact, there was only 7 other rookies that put up as many points as Puempel did goals. Puempel came out of the gate flying this year with 5 goals in his first 5 games. He did go through a short stretch where he was struggling to score, but for the most part was very consistent this season.

Puempel's main asset is his shooting skill. His slap shot is good, but his wrist shot in a main highlight due to the accuracy in which he can release it, as well as the velocity he can put on it. Puempel has shown a great ability for reading goaltenders patterns as well as showing off great accuracy. With continued work to increase his strength he can beat any goaltender at any level when he connects.

Puempel's passing abilities have been overlooked by some scouts. He has been seen connecting on high difficulty passes, most particularly on the power play. Puempel's skating has improved throughout the year, and is adequate at this point. It wouldn't be considered either an asset or a flaw. Puempel has displayed a willingness to play physical and battle for pucks. It isn't a big part of his game, but another element he does well in. He is a regular on the penalty kill in Peterborough. The biggest issue in Pumepel's game may be his consistency. There are games where he practically takes over; however, there are also several examples of him simply not showing up to games as well, and looking uninterested in the game. If he can play at his top level on a regular basis, he could be a dangerous offensive threat for years to come at the highest level. The other issue for Puempel is occasionally letting his temper get the best of him. He has been prone to using his stick inappropriately resulting in bad penalties.

Mark Scheifele

Center – Barrie Colts (OHL)
Born Mar 15 1993 - Kitchener, ONT
Height 6.02 - Weight 182 - Shoots R

HOCKEYPROSPECT.COM

ROUND ONE #24

Games	Goals	Assists	Points	PIMS	+/-
66	22	53	75	35	-22

Mark Scheifele was selected in the 7th Round of the OHL Priority Selection by the Saginaw Spirit out of the Kitchener Jr. Rangers program where he played his Minor Midget season with fellow prospect Mitchell Theoret. Scheifele chose not to report to Saginaw. Instead he remained in his hometown of Kitchener and put up impressive numbers with the Kitchener Dutchmen Jr. B team. Mark was then traded during the 2010 offseason to Barrie in a deal that sent goaltender Mavric Parks to Saginaw. The Colts were able to convince Scheifele to report and he immediately became an impact player for a Barrie team who lost several key players to graduation, trades, and the NHL.

Scheifele is a player that grew on HP scouts as the season rolled along. Mark Edwards spoke about his thoughts on him early on: "I saw him once last season and a few times early this season and he took really long shifts which put a negative vibe in my head. He showed that he had talent but was not at the same level that he finished his season at. It was his rookie season, so it's not like we don't expect an adjustment period. He skates well, sees the ice and he can both be a playmaker and goal scorer. I'll be interested to see where he gets drafted because he has been in the middle of draft rankings debates in our own meetings".

Mark has a big power forwards frame and uses it appropriately. He is an effective puck protector. He has an impressive frame but is quite lanky and will need time to fill out and get stronger. Scheifele is still a bit of a project as he needs to continue improving in the skating and shooting areas, but got a ton of exposure this year with Barrie and improved a great deal throughout the season. He projects to be a player who may need more time at the junior level to improve his skills, and grow into his frame. One thing Scheifele undoubtedly has, is a great deal of potential moving forward, and should be a valuable pick in the second half of round one, or the first half of round two.

Brett Ritchie

Right Wing – Sarnia Sting (OHL)
Born Jul 1 1993 - Orangeville, ONT
Height 6.03 - Weight 210 - Shoots R

ROUND ONE #25

Games	Goals	Assists	Points	PIMS	+/-
49	21	20	41	47	-1

Brett Ritchie was selected 12th overall by the Sarnia Sting in the 2009 OHL Priority Selection, from the Toronto Marlboros, who are also developing Brett's younger brother Nicholas, a probable top 5 pick in the 2011 OHL Priority Selection.

Brett put up 36 goals and 69 points in 71 games in Minor Midget, before making the Sarnia Sting out of training camp as a 16 year old. He posted 13 goals, and 29 points in 64 games, while receiving a fair amount of time on the 2nd line near the end of his rookie season. Ritchie continued his goal scoring success at the Ivan Hlinka tournament. He helped Canada win gold and finished 2nd in goal scoring with 4 goals in 5 games, behind only Ryan Nugent-Hopkins. Brett joined Sarnia late in the pre-season this year due to an elbow infection acquired at the end of the tournament. Ritchie started the season slowly. His goal scoring consistency has been one of his biggest problems so far in his OHL career.

Brett Ritchie has proven to be very valuable in areas that do not show up on the score sheet. Ritchie has been active along the walls and battles hard, using his size. In addition to this, Ritchie has shown the hands to both protect, and handle the puck well. He moves around the offensive zone with good vision and good control of the puck. He has also shown a capability to rush the puck up the ice through the neutral zone with authority, handling the puck well and using his size to plow through the neutral zone, and enter the attacking zone. In addition to the offensive attributes Ritchie displays, he has gradually become a more valuable defensive forward, often being the first forward back in the zone. He is adept at using his strong board play to win battles in his own zone, and get the puck out of the defensive zone. Ritchie's skating is average for someone of his size and age.

Ritchie has a good chance at becoming a prototypical Power Forward at the NHL level. Ritchie needs to work on being more physical by throwing his body around on a more consistent basis. Ritchie has a good shot at the top 50 in this year's NHL Entry Draft.

Tyler Biggs

Right Wing– USA U-18 (USHL)
Born Apr 30 1993 - Cincinnati, OH
Height 6.02 - Weight 200 Shoots -R

ROUND ONE #26

Games	Goals	Assists	Points	PIMS	+/-
48	17	11	28	112	NA

Tyler Biggs played for the HockeyPro-spect.com 1993 prospect team two springs ago. We know this player well and can vouch for him being a top notch character player to go hand in hand with his talents on the ice. HP's founder Mark Edwards on Biggs: "I'm a big fan of Tyler both as a person and as a prospect. I think Tyler is a very low risk draft pick. I'll be shocked if he does not play in the NHL. He is the type of player that every coach wants on their team. Tyler will go through a wall for his teammates. Biggs is a true 'team-first' guy who will impress NHL teams come pre-draft interview time in Toronto. Biggs' scoring touch has improved slightly, which makes his stock rise as a power forward who can also chip in on the scoreboard a little bit. NHL teams will love that he is big in stature and that he plays that way. He is tough as nails and his fighting skills have spoken for themselves over the past two seasons. I won't be shocked if Tyler ends up playing in Oshawa at some point, where his father Don played. No inside info…just a hunch."

Biggs will boost his draft stock if he can improve on his first few steps and his scoring touch. His skating is solid for a kid his size when he gets rolling. Biggs has really gained confidence in his game since scoring two goals versus Ontario to help lead USA to the gold medal in the under 17 tournament in December 2009.

We love his compete level, as Biggs hates losing a board battle let alone a hockey game. He has the ability to take over a game when he is on. When he brings his full blown nastiness he is just plain fun to watch. Biggs is a very coachable prospect who oozes upside and could easily be a top 20 pick. Biggs needs to refine his scoring skills to become an NHL top 6 forward but is a very safe bet to make the NHL and slide in as a 3rd liner.

Brandon Saad

Forward – Saginaw Spirit (OHL)
Born Oct 27 1992 - Gibsonia, PA
Height 6.01 - Weight 208 Shoots - L

ROUND ONE #27

Games	Goals	Assists	Points	PIMS	+/-
59	27	28	55	47	+8

Having a late 1992 birthdate meant Brandon Saad had to wait one more year to hear his name called at the NHL Entry Draft. Saad used that extra year to make the jump to the OHL's Saginaw spirit. Brandon ended up going 10th overall to the Saginaw Spirit. However undecided, Saad spent last year with the U.S. Development program finishing 3rd in team scoring. Brandon adapted to the OHL game very quickly, and even in pre-season, was a tough player to miss when on the ice.

Brandon is an intriguing prospect but has proven enigmatic to judge where his potential lies in the NHL. We feel Brandon is a safe pick as a future NHLer; however, his role and the capacity he will play in is a tough one to grasp at this point. Proven primarily due to his outstanding play in the first half of the season, then the way he fell off as the January and February months hit.

Brandon appeared to be on a high, scoring 12 goals in 12 games from late October to the end of November. However he dropped off in January and February scoring only 1 goal over 12 games. Saad is a player highlighted by his great combination of a big frame, and good skating abilities. He has a solid stride combined with good acceleration and has shown the ability to break away from opposing players when given space. In scoring his goals earlier in the season, Saad did so showing good hand/eye coordination, and the ability to unload a solid shot even from awkward places. Although his skating is strong he's not extremely agile, so he utilizes his puck protection abilities to fend off defensive players as he drives towards the goal.

Saad has also shown very quickly at the OHL level his strong defensive game. Brandon teamed up with Vincent Trocheck as a regular forward pairing on the penalty kill. He is effective in his own zone, and a threat to take the puck the other way for short-handed scoring opportunities. Going forward Saad will need to be more physical as he has the frame and strength to do so, and bring his "A" game for the entire season, as he faded off top 10 radar's as the season progressed.

Ryan Sproul

Defense – Soo Greyhounds (OHL)
Born Jan 13 1993 - Mississauga, ONT
Height 6.04 - Weight 190 - Shoots R

Games	Goals	Assists	Points	PIMS	+/-
61	14	19	33	36	-15

Ryan Sproul is an interesting prospect. He start-started this season with the Vaughan Vipers Junior 'A' team and had HP's founder, Mark Edwards, as his defense coach.

Edwards had this to say about Sproul: "I spent the summer watching Ryan improve. I knew we had him signed with Vaughan and he played on my summer team as well as taking part in our various Vipers camps and skates. Sproul impressed me right away with his tools. He was raw as far as the defensive zone play goes, but was making progress in that area. His shot was fantastic and his skating was good. His offensive instincts were high end. He had a knack for knowing when to jump into the play, and when he did, he was explosive and he made things happen. He played very well in his brief stay with Vaughan. We had a pretty good idea we would lose him despite interest from Michigan and other schools. I was disappointed at his lack of opportunity early on with the Greyhounds. I knew he could really contribute right away with his offensive abilities. It was nice to see him get a chance to show what he could do later in the season. He has improved in all areas of his game. The biggest improvement for me is that he showed a lack of intensity at times and he has really changed that part of his game. He shows much more fire in his game from shift to shift. He was a coachable and likeable kid. It's always enjoyable to send players off to bigger and better things."

Sproul finally got his chance in the Soo and showed the coaches that he could run an OHL pow-erplay. He put up Ryan Murphy/Ryan Ellis type goal numbers once he was finally given some decent ice time and special teams ice. His game improved in all areas. He got much better in his own zone and through the neutral zone and started to read the play much better defensively. He arrived in the Soo with great offensive instincts and he got even better as he gained experience and confidence. We saw Sproul as a huge dark horse right from the get-go this season. We would not be totally shocked if he is scooped up at the end of the 1st round. If he slides into day two, we don't expect him to be sitting in his seat in the Xcel Energy Center very long.

Tomas Jurco

Right Wing – Saint John Sea Dogs (QMJHL)
Born Dec 28 1992 - Kosice, Slovakia
Height 6.02 - Weight 187 - Shoots L

Games	Goals	Assists	Points	PIMS	+/-
60	31	25	56	17	+46

If you want a game breaker, a magician with the puck, an elite skilled forward, this Slovakian is just what you need. He plays the most exciting brand of hockey that fans just love. He may not be every coach's cup of tea, but he can certainly help give his team a better chance to win every night with the tools he has in his toolbox.

Tomas Jurco has a good frame at 6'02" 193 pounds, yet he's one of the most agile players with the puck in the CHL. His talent is undeniable and he can undress any defenseman when he's on his game. He has really good speed and great vision of the whole ice. He makes difficult plays look easy, has a top-level skillset and creates a lot of opportunities for his teammates. He has a good hard wrist shot that is released quickly and also a good one-timer slap shot. He's a real threat with time and space and a specialist in situations like the powerplay. He's learning the defensive game. It's a work in progress and both he and Jonathan Huberdeau put forth a good amount of effort in that facet of the game.

Jurco still needs to simplify his game. He can be prone to dangle too much at times and creates some poor turnovers that could easily be avoided. At times, when the other team plays a more defensive style of game he needs to chip and chase the puck when the situation requires it. He needs to pick up those garbage goals and be a better presence in front of the net. He needs to adjust his European game a bit more to the North American style. With his skill, if he does tweak his game a bit, he'll be one heck of a game breaker in the NHL. Work ethic is not missing from this young forward. Jurco is a very solid prospect for this year's draft.

Vlady Namestnikov

Center – London Knights (OHL)
Born Nov 22 1992 - Russia
Height 6.00 - Weight 170 - Shoots L

ROUND ONE #30

Games	Goals	Assists	Points	PIMS	+/-
68	30	38	68	49	+12

Vladislav Namestnikov is widely considered the top Russian for the 2011 NHL Entry Draft. Namestnikov was developed by his home club Khimik Voskresensk, and played in the Russian 2nd league last year, but after being selected 20th overall by the London Knights in the CHL Import Draft, the Knights were able to persuade Namestnikov to the CHL. Namestnikov has plenty of NHL experience in his bloodlines with former fellow CHL Import Draftee and NHL'er Ivan Novoseltsev, and longtime NHL'er Vyacheslav (Slava) Kozlov to call his uncles.

Namestnikov started out slowly in the OHL, adjusting to the North American game, and still is a very streaky player. He displays a slight frame, and although he handles physicality well for an 18 year old import player, he needs to gain more strength. Without question Namestnikov's greatest skill is his skating ability. He has a great top speed, and his acceleration from standing position is arguably one of the best in this draft class. He is one of those rare players who looks even faster with the puck than without it. He is a very elusive and shifty player. He is very hard to slow down, and is surprisingly hard to knock off the puck considering his frame. He is very good in 1 on 1 situations off the rush and coming off the half-boards.

Namestnikov's offensive awareness is very strong, as is his positional play on the power play. Along with his individual skills, Namestnikov also distributes the puck very well. If he chooses to remain in North America he has a good chance at one day playing in a top 6 role in the NHL. Despite having great hands Namestnikov's shot needs to improve a bit, which will come with him hitting the weight room on a more consistent basis. Although listed as a Right Winger, Namestnikov can play all three forward positions, and plays Center far more than any other. Namestnikov has had a fair amount of success in the face-off circle this year. Namestnikov needs to really work hard to improve his defensive zone coverage. He has been a liability in that area at times this season.

Dmitri Jaskin

Right Wing – Slavia, (CZREP)
Born Mar 23 1993, Czech Republic
Height 6.01 -- Weight 196 – Shoots L

Games	Goals	Assists	Points	PIMS	+/-
33	3	7	10	16	NA

We were looking forward to getting a good long look at Jaskin in Buffalo at the World Junior Championship, but an injury messed that up. We would have liked to have been able to compare him to other Euros competing against the same competition.

Much like a Zach Bell, Jaskin is not going to have you raving about how pretty a skater he is. But, like Bell, Jaskin is deceptively fast. He will never be a winner of a foot speed award, but he just gets it done. The thing we like about Jaskin is he plays what many would call "a North American game". Jaskin plays a power forward game but has top 6 skills to go along with it. His shot is high end and his release even better, as it's lightning quick. We talk a lot about players who are willing to go to the dirty areas of the ice. You can add Dmitri to that list of players. Jaskin is a fierce competitor and has a really good work ethic. Coaches are always telling players to go to the net. Jaskin seemed to get this message. Last year we told you that Jared Knight went hard to the net. You can put Jaskin in that class or possibly better - he is bigger to boot.

Jaskin impressed us as a smart player. He is crafty working along the walls and wins battles on a regular basis. He does a good job working the puck down low and understands the cycle game. He understands the value of puck possession and waits until he has a good option with the puck before just throwing it into a high risk area. His vision and smarts are that of 1st round material.

As we said, His foot speed is not very good. He has a sluggish and ugly first few steps. Guess what? So did Ryan O'Reilly and we ranked him higher than anyone did. We expect a team to grab Jaskin in the 1st round. His recent showing in Germany did nothing but raise his stock.

Nicklas Jensen

LW/RW – Oshawa Generals (OHL)
Born Mar 16 1993 - Herning, Denmark
Height 6.02 - Weight 188 - Shoots L

Games	Goals	Assists	Points	PIMS	+/-
61	29	29	58	42	+14

Players at all levels battle through confidence issues at some point in their careers. The ones that work to overcome tentativeness become top-flight professionals. Others, even talented players, may fade into obscurity. Many scouts are hoping Norwegian winger Nicklas Jensen does not suffer this fate. He has all the tools to be a good NHL player, including size and high-end skills. He has put up solid numbers for Oshawa in the Ontario Hockey League.

At 6-foot-3 and 190 pounds, Jensen has great mobility for his size. He is not a skater with blazing speed, but he possesses excellent quickness and burst. His offensive skills are terrific as well. Jensen is not afraid to take on defenders and has superior 1-on-1 ability. But the trait that makes Jensen an intriguing prospect is his lightning-quick wrist shot. He is a pure goal scorer, and his shot is heavy and accurate. While he does not always use his great size to his advantage, Jensen is able to find the quiet areas of the ice. He uses his puck skills to maneuver around defenders and score highlight-reel goals. Battling on the boards is a strength, but continued improvement on his physical game will only make Jensen harder to play against.

Jensen is not a great passer and needs to work on his engagement level. Whether it is a confidence issue or just floating around, Jensen will need to be more assertive to be effective in the NHL. Defensively, Jensen leaves a lot to be desired. He is prone to mental lapses in the defense zone. When he is truly engaged, he looks like a promising two-way winger. When he hesitates and does not join the play, he becomes invisible at times. This may hurt his draft stock, but with his offensive skills and size, Jensen is a promising prospect.

Nick Cousins

Center/Wing – Soo Greyhounds (OHL)
Born Jul 20 1993 - Belleville, ONT
Height 5.11 - Weight 166 - Shoots L

ROUND TWO #33

Games	Goals	Assists	Points	PIMS	+/-
68	29	39	68	56	-14

Nick Cousins was the first player selected in the 2nd round of the 2009 OHL Priority Selection by the Sault Ste. Marie Greyhounds. Cousins fell to the Greyhounds despite being touted as a 1st round prospect in this draft out of the Quinte Red Devils program. Cousins not only made the team out of camp as a 16 year old, but actually outperformed 1st Overall pick Daniel Catenacci in goals, assists, and points. Also, he was at times the more visible prospect. This season Cousins has settled into an important role with the team, playing all game situations.

Cousins uses his vision and awareness to anticipate the play on the ice and acquire good positioning. Cousins has some of the most underrated hands in the goal area among draft eligible prospects. Cousins also works hard down low, and has the ability to make difficult passes in order to set up offense. He also has a good accurate shot which he has used to help improve his goal totals this season.

Cousins has faired pretty well when going 1 on 1 with opposing defenders. He has a solid top speed, but his acceleration needs improvement. Cousins, who is not always noticeable, does a lot of the little things right for his team. He works hard along the boards and contributes in all 3 zones. Cousins has also shown fairly well in the face-off circle. Nick has a solid work ethic and with his array of talents, might be one of the better selections in the 2011 NHL Entry Draft who doesn't get talked about very much.

Cousins has been a player we really liked going back to his minor hockey days. He helped raise his stock to the masses with a very strong U18 tournament in Germany in April.

Daniel Catenacci

Center – Soo Greyhounds (OHL)
Born Mar 9 1993 - Richmond Hill, ONT
Height 5.10 - Weight 183 - Shoots L

Games	Goals	Assists	Points	PIMS	+/-
67	25	46	71	117	-5

Daniel Catenacci was selected 1st overall in the 2009 OHL Priority Selection by the Sault Ste. Marie Greyhounds out of the York-Simcoe Express program. Catenacci entered the league with a lot of hype, and had a bit of a disappointing rookie season, not showing the potential that was expected out of him. There were a lot of question marks surrounding how Catenacci would follow up his sophomore season. Some rankings saw him start out fairly low; however, Catenacci started out strong, and has doubled his goals, assists and points totals from last season.

Catenacci is highlighted by his outstanding skating ability. Catenacci has a very strong lower body, and seems to absorb contact that is not directly head on, and displays exceptional acceleration and balance. Combined with great shiftiness, he is one of the most difficult prospects to stop 1 on 1. Catenacci has solid offensive instincts. He has shown on numerous occasions to be able to create offense for both himself and his teammates, and is willing to give up the puck when the opportunity arises. Catenacci has shown the ability to play physical and take physicality. He is a gritty forward willing to get his hands dirty, and willing to take the hit to make the play. Catenacci is fairly responsible defensively and effective on the PK. Daniel has also has shown on multiple occasions a willingness to block shots.

Consistency will ultimately play a huge part in judging Daniel Catenacci, as he had two major streaks during the season. Daniel played on a weak team all season long and was not helped by stretches where the Greyhounds rolled 4 lines outside of special teams. We saw stretches where Catenacci would see as few as one 5 on 5 shift in a period. In games where the Greyhounds took multiple penalties, he really lacked 5 on 5 ice time and extended tons of energy killing penalties.

Will Daniel be a legitimate smallish top six forward in the NHL? Or will he be a speedy bottom six role player with some offensive upside? It's a good sign that he can be considered for both roles and makes him less of a boom or bust type of prospect.

Jonathan Miller

Center – USA U-18 (USHL)
Born March 14, 1993 East Palestine, OH
Height 6.01 - Weight - 198 - Shoots L

Games	Goals	Assists	Points	PIMS	+/-
48	11	26	37	78	NA

J.T Miller is a University of North Dakota recruit and one of the more interesting stories on draft day could be where J.T Miller gets picked. Miller has tools but has not been able to find the toolbox on a regular basis.

Miller skates well and gets up to full speed quickly for a big kid. His feet are pretty quick and he is actually very agile, especially for a 200 pounder. We're not sure he has the type of speed to pull away from defenders but again, we don't consider skating to be one of his weaknesses. He has the size to play in the NHL and that frame of his should only fill out more, which makes him more attractive to NHL teams. He is very solid in many aspects of the game. He protects the puck, is a horse along the walls, and wins battles on a regular basis. He goes hard to the net and is not afraid to go to the dirty areas to get pucks or screen a goalie. Miller likes to throw his body around and he is an athletic player. His puck skills are also very good. J.T could be described as having very good hands and stick-handling ability. He shows off some pretty decent moves at times. He forechecks well but this can be one of those areas where he lacks the consistency any scout wants to see out of a player.

So what's not to like right? Well this is a prospect that can make scouts lose their jobs. J.T's numbers just don't seem to add up to totals you would expect when you see the tools he has to work with. Our take is that he lacks some vision and high end hockey smarts to be a top six guy in the NHL. He might even end up being on the outside looking in for an NHL roster spot. At the end of the day, this is a player who makes scouts earn their money. Is he a player who indeed does have what it takes to play on one of the top two lines of an NHL team? Or is Miller not quite there yet when it comes to little things that make good players great? We are a bit scared off by the 11 goals in 48 games. We think it's a bit risky to bet the farm on him as a 1st round talent at this point in his development. We hope he proves us wrong.

Stefan Noesen

Right Wing – Plymouth Whalers (OHL)
Born Feb 12 1993 - Plano, TX
Height 6.00 - Weight 195 - Shoots R

Games	Goals	Assists	Points	PIMS	+/-
68	34	43	77	480	+14

Few players show the type of two-way promise that NHL teams covet at such a young age. Stefan Noesen of the Plymouth Whalers is one of the few. Known as more of a defensive forward, Noesen has developed a nice offensive game this season. He is a terrific passer and shows promise with his goal scoring ability. He is a puck hound and tenacious forechecker as well. He is not afraid to lay the body and finishes all of his checks. Although Noesen's skating is not poor, he will need to work on quickness and agility to further improve his game.

Noesen is exceptional with respect to defensive positioning. He has a very high hockey IQ and knows where to be on the ice. Noesen rarely gets caught out of position and battles for pucks along the boards with a resolute attitude. His smarts coupled with a superb work ethic have led to a vast improvement over the course of the season. Noesen has moved from a bottom-six forward to one of the more reliable players on the team. He is continuously one of the hardest working players on the ice every night. His size at 6-foot-1 and 195 pounds makes his physical play that much more effective. Noesen makes sure that his presence is felt, not only with his physicality, but forcing defenseman to make quick passes. This pressure creates a number of turnovers.

HP is excited about Noesen's upside. With improved skating, he has the ability to make an impact in the NHL. He will only get bigger and stronger in the coming years. Because he has improved so much over the past few seasons, there is no reason to believe his learning curve will slow down. Noesen could be a steal come draft day because of his work ethic, responsible play in all three zones, and ideal size and skill.

Zack Phillips

Center– Saint John Sea Dogs (QMJHL)
Born Oct 28 1992 - Fredericton, NB
Height 6.01 - Weight 178 - Shoots R

Games	Goals	Assists	Points	PIMS	+/-
67	38	57	95	16	+48

Phillips is an interesting player because his stats are probably boosted a bit by the packed lineup in St-John, but he still brings a different asset to the table.

Phillips, who has late 1992 birthday plays a grinding game with impressive offensive talent. He's a strong kid and he has a contrasting style compared to the other highly skilled forwards in Saint-John. He likes to keep the puck on the boards, use his strength and speed to battle defensemen one on one and crash the net pretty hard. He likes to get his nose dirty and he's still pretty disciplined while doing so. His skating is his biggest weakness. He gets a lot of his chances by simply having good position on the ice and knowing how to get himself free from defensive coverage. He has good skills with the puck even though he's not a really shifty player, but he can still twist and turn pretty good with the puck. He's willing to sacrifice his body to make plays in his own zone and he's not afraid to block shots.

He's pretty good in his own zone but needs to see the play develop a bit better and run around a bit less. He's aggressive down low, but can get caught and we have seen that happen a couple of times with Zach Phillips. We would like to see him use his body a little bit more to give good body checks especially on the forecheck. He has good effort chasing the puck-possessing player but he needs to use his body a bit more to neutralize them. He would also benefit if he had a bit more acceleration in his skating in order to create more scoring chances when moving through the neutral zone and going wide on defensemen.

Skating issues may turn out to be the stopper for Phillips in the NHL and is the reason we dropped him a bit in our rankings. He is very talented in just about every other area of his game.

John Gibson

Goalie – USNTDP (USHL)
Born Jul 14 1993 - Pittsburgh, PA
Height 6.03 - Weight 205 – Catches L

Games	Wins	Losses	G.A.A	Save %	SO
32	17	10	2.64	.918	1

Like his predecessor Jack Campbell last year, United States National Team Development Program goalie John Gibson is one of the best in this year's class. With bigger goalies becoming the craze in the NHL today, Gibson's size is a huge asset. At 6-foot-3 and 185 pounds, Gibson covers a lot of the net. He will undoubtedly fill out his frame in the coming years. While his size is certainly noticeable, his skills are what have scouts excited.

He is a very good athlete. He has great agility, and his post-to-post movement is exceptional. Gibson is a very competitive netminder and plays at the top of the crease. He does not get caught sagging in the paint and bury himself in the net. This allows him to cut down on shooting angles and remain in solid position. Although he is a great athlete, his technical skills are very good as well. He does not flail around in the net very often and seems to react quickly while remaining in good position. His rebound control is also quite good, something many young goalies struggle with.

Gibson has committed to play at the University of Michigan. College competition will season the youngster, and with Michigan's streak of NCAA tournament appearances, he will likely get to play in many pressure-packed games. Gibson does not shy away from the spotlight and seems to shine when the stage is biggest. He was excellent in the Five Nation's tournament in February. Although HP is not big on selecting goalies in the first round, Gibson's size, skill, poise and competitiveness make him a very good prospect that could hear his name called early come June.

Rocco Grimaldi

Forward – USNTDP (USHL)
Born Feb 8 1993 - Auburn Hills, MI
Height 5.06 - Weight 163 Shoots - R

ROUND TWO #39

Games	Goals	Assists	Points	PIMS	+/-
50	34	28	62	57	NA

Determination is just one of the traits that teams look at when selecting a player. A franchise wants players that have the will to fiercely compete and win, not guys that routinely take shifts off. It would be difficult to find a player in this draft class that epitomizes determination as much as Rocco Grimaldi. In 32 games with the United States National Team Development Program's U17 squad last season, Grimaldi netted 11 goals and 20 points.

At just 5-foot-6 and 165 pounds, Grimaldi has to overcome a major lack of size to compete at a high level. But the diminutive forward does just that. Through 38 games this season, he leads the USNTDP's U18 team in scoring with 24 goals and 45 points. As one might expect, Grimaldi neutralizes his smaller stature with a high hockey IQ and terrific skills. He is a phenomenal skater that exemplifies what it means to use the edges of the skates, thus giving Grimaldi a smooth stride, explosive quickness and exceptional balance. That speed is coupled with dynamic offensive instincts. Grimaldi is a pure goal scorer, and he has a very powerful shot despite his size. He has a lightning-quick release as well. Grimaldi is equally adept as a passer, and his vision is outstanding. He has a flare for the dramatic as well, by scoring timely goals. He possesses a great motor and works extremely hard to make an impact on every shift, something that makes him a commodity for any team.

Grimaldi will need to continue his tireless work ethic if he hopes to succeed at the NHL level. Players like Tampa Bay's Martin St. Louis prove that you can be effective in the NHL even with a small stature. Grimaldi is headed to the University of North Dakota next season to continue his development. Working with one of the top programs in college hockey should help prepare the forward to take his game to the next level. Possible boom or bust potential kept him out of our 1st round. He is a player that we openly accept may end up making us look bad.

Matt Nieto

LW – Boston University (NCAA)
Born Nov 5 1992 - Long Beach, CA
Height 5.10 - Weight 175 - Shoots L

Games	Goals	Assists	Points	PIMS	+/-
39	10	13	23	16	-3

Nieto joined the ranks of California-born players such as 2010's Emerson Etem and Beau Bennett. Nieto looks to be a fairly high draft pick out of the sunshine state. A left winger for NCAA-powerhouse Boston University, Nieto has solid size. He is not very tall, but is built well and should only get bigger with plenty of time to work out at the NCAA level. Nieto had a tough adjustment to the NCAA level, especially with BU in a re-building year, but came on very strong as the season went along, and ended up with impressive stats for a true freshman. Nieto is arguably the top player in BU's freshman class and should take on an even bigger role next season as he looks to make a World Junior push.

Nieto jumps out at you with his speed the first time you watch him. He can really move and gets to his top speed in a hurry. He has good creativity but far too often let's himself get skated into lower percentage scoring areas. Matt has the ability to be an explosive player and has shown this ability at the NCAA level. The key for his draft day will be how much faith scouts put in him to bring it up yet another notch next season, as he did towards the second half of this season.

It's hard to look past a player with the skating ability of Nieto. He is not just a burner with a good burst. Our favorite part about his game is the agility he shows on his edges in tight areas. This makes him tougher to handle in 1 on 1 battles. We don't have a problem with his work ethic. In fact, it's another strong part of his game. His shot and release are also at a high level. A weakness might be his awareness in his own zone, and at times even in his neutral zone play. Nieto could be an early 2nd day pick and worst case should be picked up before you need to stretch your legs on Saturday morning.

Christopher Gibson

Goalie – Chicoutimi (QMJHL)
Born Dec 27 1992, Karkkila, FIN
Height 6.01 - Weight 198 - Catches L

ROUND TWO #41

Games	Wins	Losses	G.A.A	Save %	SO
37	14	15	2.42	.920	4

Gibson played his final Midget hockey season in Saskatchewan with Notre Dame as he came from Finland to play the Canadian style of hockey before he was eligible for the CHL Import Draft. Christopher Gibson was selected by Chicoutimi. He made an immediate impact on the Chicoutimi Saguenéens last season, helping the team come back from a 1-3 deficit in the playoffs to a losing effort in the series, 4-3 in overtime against a much stronger Rimouski team. He made some real clutch saves then and he has been the best goalie in the CHL so far this season, making the key saves the Chicoutimi squad needs to get wins.

What makes Gibson so good is his attitude. He is focused for 60 minutes and he never seems to lose that focus whether he gets run into or if he gives up a bad goal, which doesn't happen a lot. Everything he does seems cool and calm. He makes tough saves look pretty easy because he does every movement with perfect technique. He has good reflexes and a quick glove to save pucks even after a deflection. He likes to go behind his net and he needs improvement in this area. It is something he wants to incorporate in his game. He has good size, and he can make good saves through traffic because he challenges the shooters high, outside of his crease which makes the saves look even easier sometimes. He has good rebound control and great flexibility to make post to post saves.

Christopher Gibson needs to work on stopping breakaways. He needs to be more aggressive on the shooters and adjust his speed correctly to the shooter's pace. He also needs to improve more on lateral movements and gain more strength in his legs. In pro hockey, passes come faster and if he can get quicker in these movements, with the technique he has, he'll be an elite goalie wherever he plays. He has great quick legs, but he needs more quickness on his post to post movements.

Samu Perhonen

Goalie– JYP JR. (FINLAND-JR)
Born Mar 7 1993 - Jamsankoski
Height 6.04 - Weight 172 - Catches L

Games	Wins	Losses	G.A.A	Save %	SO
29	NA	NA	2.71	.922	2

Samu Perhonen has emerged as the best goaltending prospect out of Europe for the 2011 NHL Entry Draft. Playing for JYP's junior program, which most recently developed Anaheim Ducks prospect defenseman Sami Vatanen, this big Finnish netminder has been coming up through the ranks, and was one of the top goaltenders in the U20 league, despite being only 17 for much of the season. Perhonen took over the starting role for Finland at the U18's and did a respectable job keeping his team in most games.

Perhonen is very technically sound, and is fairly quick for a goaltender with outstanding size, which gives him a solid frame to build upon. Perhonen doesn't do one thing exceptionally well, and on the other side of that, he doesn't have any glaring flaws in his game.

Samu is fairly complete, and should he take the appropriate steps in his development, he could turn into a very solid and very big goaltender. Perhonen would be an attractive option for the CHL Import Draft; however, it appears he would prefer to stay in Finland, and possibly earn a spot with JYP's Top level team, and play against men, which would certainly be a big test for the big netminder.

Like most goaltenders drafted, Perhonen probably won't be rushed and it will be years before the drafting team finds out if their draft selection pans out., However, Samu is considered "next in line" in terms of the great goaltenders Finland has developed. Look for years of development, but Perhonen is off to a great start, and he's just now turned 18 years old.

Gregory Hofmann

LW/Center – Ambri, (SWISS)
Born Mar 9 1993 - Switzerland
Height 6.00 - Weight 170 - Shoots L

Games	Goals	Assists	Points	PIMS	+/-
41	3	9	12	2	NA

We really liked Hofmann at the World Juniors in Buffalo. He stood out to us in every game with his smart play and work ethic. Hofmann made so many good decisions with the puck it was hard for him not to stand out to us.

Hofmann showed playmaking ability and an understanding of where to be in all three zones. His passing skills were good and he should the ability to create and also to take the smart simple play when it was the best choice. He competed in all three zones as well as anyone on his team. Greg shows no fear and a willingness to go into dirty areas.

Hofmann is a good skater, he seems solid on his skates and when he adds some strength to his legs and upper body his whole game will hit a new level. In summary, this kid is not far off first round talent.

We see him as a very smart, hard working forward that gets after it. He showed off the skills of a high level draft pick. Hofmann will be a player that we follow closely at the NHL Draft this year. When we were watching him during the World Junior's in Buffalo, he grew on us more with each shift we watched. He didn't show off the skills of his teammate, Sven Baertschi, but he showed loads of heart and desire. He came across to us as a player that any coach would trust in any situation. Hofmann had that certain 'it' factor that any team needs in a player and of course, searches for.

We don't know when Hofmann will come off the board in Minnesota this June but we are confident that the team drafting him will get a good hockey player. A big factor may be his willingness or possibly a lack thereof to make the trip to North America like his countrymen and compete in the CHL. When I spoke to Swiss National coach, Sean Simpson, during the World Jr's tournament, he gave me the indication that he liked the development that both Niederreiter and Sven Bartschi have seen in their games. Hofmann showed us enough to value him as a second round draft pick.

Lucas Lessio

Left Wing – Oshawa Generals (OHL)
Born Jan 23 1993 - Maple, ONT
Height 6.01 - Weight 196 - Shoots L

Games	Goals	Assists	Points	PIMS	+/-
66	27	27	54	66	+8

Lucas Lessio was a standout winger for the Toronto Marlboros, which saw him drafted 7th overall by the Niagara Ice Dogs, and first out of a talented group from the Marlboros' program which also included Ryan Strome, Brett Ritchie, and Stuart Percy. Lessio decided to weigh his options, thus reporting to St. Michael's Buzzers while he made his decision. Lessio exceled for St. Michael's putting up big points. Lessio's rights were traded from Niagara to Oshawa, where after some deliberation, Lucas joined the Generals.

The highlight of Lessio's skill set appears to be his compete level. He always seems to have energy to spare. He takes pride in being one of the hardest workers on the ice and in his ability to fly into the dirty areas without hesitation. Lessio does an excellent job battling in the corners.

Lessio's skating was exposed a bit when we saw him early on the big ice in Belleville, but it seems throughout the year his skating has got better on almost a weekly basis. Elusiveness was never a question, however he is at the point now that combined with his great stick handling abilities, his acceleration gets him to top speed quickly, and helps him break away after making a great move. Although Lessio always seems to have a close goal to assist ratio, you can see him looking pass. When he does decide to shoot Lessio has an excellent release, and is very dangerous in the goal area.

Lessio is a player with few flaws. He is not exceptional in any particular area. He hits, battles in corners, shoots, passes, and protects his own zone. Although he has some enigmatic traits to him, we expect Lucas to remain on the path of a solid NHL prospect.

Michael St. Croix

Center – Edmonton Oil Kings (WHL)
Born Apr 10 1993 - Winnipeg, MAN
Height 5.11 - Weight 176 - Shoots R

ROUND TWO #45

Games	Goals	Assists	Points	PIMS	+/-
68	27	48	75	48	+28

St.Croix has very good vision which serves him well, putting the puck through the smallest holes to find his teammate's stick.. Mike is more than just a solid playmaker, he can put the puck in the net as well. Michael St. Croix was drafted 4th overall by the Edmonton Oil Kings, and has shown off his offensive skills. As a 15 year old he scored a goal, and added an assist in two games. Then as a 16 year old rookie, he put up 18 goals and 46 points. St. Croix has lead the Oil Kings in assists the past 2 years as a tribute to his playmaking abilities. We also interviewed Michael last summer and he was one of the best interviews we have ever done. He impressed us with his responses.

St. Croix has very good vision which helps him put the puck through the smallest lanes to find his teammates stick. He is excellent in the playmaking department. This may be the biggest factor that drastically affects his willingness to shoot the puck, as he has one of the fastest catch and releases of any prospect we've seen for this year's draft. He will go from receiving a pass, to putting it in the back of the net incredibly quick.

He is dangerous in the offense zone, not only because of his passing and shooting skills, but he's fairly elusive. His physical game is inconsistent. We have seen come out of the corners with the puck during a battle, but at other times he appears like he doesn't want to get hit, and will pass the puck up in order to avoid contact. St. Croix has shown strong skating ability, and is fairly shifty. He has made some nice moves 1 on 1, and is capable of scoring highlight reel goals.. Michael will need to overcome his size to succeed at the next level; however, he has the intangibles that make that a good possibility. He also needs to get stronger, and be more willing to engage physically on a regular basis. He doesn't need to become a physical player, but needs to do away with the occasional timid play we've seen in his game. In the NHL the bigger and stronger defensemen will really expose that weakness.

Victor Rask

Center – Leksand (SWE)
Born March 1 1993 - Leksand, SWE
Height 6.02 - Weight 194 - Shoots L

Games	Goals	Assists	Points	PIMS	+/-
37	5	6	11	8	NA

One of the more frustrating things for scouts is to watch a player with terrific skills perform in a wildly inconsistent fashion. In a nutshell, that is Swedish center Victor Rask. He has dominated the junior leagues in Sweden at times with his terrific skills. When it comes to pure ability, Rask is most certainly near the top of this year's draft class. Rask's problems lie with his enigmatic play that leaves scouts wondering why he does not dominate even more.

He has terrific size at 6-foot-2 and 190 pounds. He wins battles in the Swedish junior leagues but will need to use his size much more frequently to have any chance in the NHL. Like many Europeans, his puck skills are second to none. He makes highlight-reel plays out of nothing with his creativity. Rask's skating is questionable, and he does not have great speed or quickness. He makes up for his sluggish skating with solid decision making. Rask is prone to being a bit selfish with the puck but makes plays nonetheless. He is adept at setting up teammates but does not display those skills as frequently as he needs to. Adjusting to the North American game might be difficult for Rask as his two-way game leaves a lot to be desired. He is weak defensively and will need strong schooling to be an impact player in the NHL.

While the 18-year-old has plenty of time to iron out the wrinkles in his game, he needs to make a concerted effort to work harder. This will determine whether Rask becomes a good NHL player or plays in Europe for the rest of his career. Despite his weaknesses, Rask remains a highly-touted prospect based on his skill alone. Putting the pieces of his game together could allow Rask to become a top-flight offensive talent at the NHL level.

Xavier Ouellet

Defense– Montreal Juniors (QMJHL)
Born Jul 29 1993 - Terrebonne, PQ
Height 6.01 - Weight 177 - Shoots L

ROUND TWO #47

Games	Goals	Assists	Points	PIMS	+/-
67	8	35	43	44	+27

Xavier Ouellet is the number one defenseman on a veteran squad with the Montreal Juniors, a team that is targeting the Memorial Cup this season. He has been rock solid in his own zone and he's been able to play in all kinds of situations because of his speed and intelligence on the ice.

He's always moving his feet and he is really solid in his own zone. His gap control is very good and he shows a good active stick on opponents. He's not overly physical or aggressive, but he knows how to position himself to be in the face of opposing players.

Ouellet has good passing skills and it would seem that he likes to join the rush a couple of times per game. His maturity on the ice gives the opportunity for coach Pascal Vincent to play him in every situation. He is a smart hockey player and that's the most impressive thing with Ouellet. He looks like a veteran on the ice, but he's just 17 years old. He sees the ice pretty well and he opens up passing lanes giving himself options with his quick feet.

The biggest flaw for Xavier Ouellet is his shot. He doesn't seem to have confidence in it because he never shoots it. He doesn't like to slide to the middle of the ice to take shots. He has a good low wrist shot that he could use more often to create rebounds for his forwards. Overall strength can be an issue for some scouts. We think it's going to come naturally for Xavier and he'll surely win more 1-on-1 battles when this strength increases. With the incredible maturity he shows in all situations at only 17 of age, you can't deny this young gun has a certain something. We expected a bit more from Ouellet this year but the kid is still young and he had a good year. His skating will help him reach the next level. If he starts to step it up a bit with his physical play, it will raise his chances of playing in the NHL. We spoke to Montreal head coach Pascal Vincent on two different occasions this season regarding separate topics. It was interesting that the conversations managed to swing towards Xavier both times. Pascal could not say enough positive things about the young defenseman.

Alex Khokhlachev

LW/Center – Windsor Spitfires (OHL)
Born Sep 9 1993 - Moscow, Russia
Height 5.10 - Weight 188 - Shoots L

HOCKEYPROSPECT.COM

ROUND TWO #48

Games	Goals	Assists	Points	PIMS	+/-
67	34	42	76	28	+9

Like many Russian players, Windsor Spitfires forward Alexander Khokhlachev has superior skills and the personality to go with it. He is an energetic player with skill to boot. Khokhlachev was a member of the Russian Junior League before coming to the Ontario Hockey League and Windsor. His transition to the North American game was very smooth. Although he does not have great size at 5-foot-10 and 185 pounds, Khokhlachev has a motor that never stops running.

Khokhlachev plays a high-energy game on most nights. One of the things we don't like about him is that he has been a no show in too many games. We saw games where he really impressed and others where we had to double check to make sure he wasn't a scratch. He is very strong on the fore-check and back-check. Like fellow Russian Pavel Datsyuk, Khokhlachev plays a smart two-way game, a trait that will endear him to many NHL teams. With the ability to play either wing or center, Khokhlachev will provide versatility to any lineup. He is very creative offensively and is equally adept as a passer or shooter. We would like to see him play less on the perimeter and get more involved along the walls. Like most players with a smaller stature, he is an excellent skater with speed, quickness, and elusiveness. Although he does not have eye-popping size, his frame is built well enough to withstand punishment. Khokhlachev's size and strength will certainly improve in the coming years.

When he's on, his work ethic is extremely impressive. With his speed, skill and determination, he is a good prospect. The concerns we have with Alex are that while he works hard he can shy away from the dirty areas at times. Alex needs to go hard after loose pucks more often and show more willingness to battle. The other concern is his lack of consistency from game to game.

Connor Murphy

Defense – USNTDP (USHL)
Born Mar 26 1993 - Boston, MA
Height 6.03 - Weight 185 - Shoots R

ROUND TWO #49

Games	Goals	Assists	Points	PIMS	+/-
14	3	3	6	6	NA

Connor Murphy battled a back injury and had his season limited to just 14 games this season. Murphy managed to post six points in those 14 games including 3 goals. The son of former NHL'er Gord Murphy might be one of the players who helped out his draft stock as much as anyone in the recently completed U18 Tourney in Germany. Murphy showed us more ability and smarts than we expected all tournament long, to go along with some really good offensive upside.

Connor was forced to show his stuff to a huge number of scouts in Germany without the benefit of a full season of extra development in his hip pocket. To his credit, he had little trouble impressing and therefore raising his draft stock heading into June.

We loved his play all over the ice. In the neutral zone and on rushes he showed a tight gap and used his stick well to poke away pucks. He played a consistently smart brand of hockey. Murphy read plays very well and put himself in position to break up plays all over the ice.

When draft day rolls around Murphy's play in the U -18's in Germany will surely help his play. He played very sound, smart hockey and showed scouts that he has a good idea of how the position is supposed to be played. This is an impressive part of Connor's game when you factor in how few games he has played over the last two years. Of course, with the good comes the bad, and injuries play a part into draft position.

When all is said and done we feel that more than any other factor, Murphy's past injury woes will keep his draft stock out of round 1 and closer to a middle of the pack round 2 pick.

Mario Lucia

Left Wing – Wayzata (H.S Minnesota)
Born Aug 25, 1993 - Fairbanks, Alaska
Height 6.02 - Weight 183 - Shoots L

Games	Goals	Assists	Points	PIMS	+/-
24	25	22	47	14	NA

There are always a few players that shoot up the draft boards during the course of the season. Winger Mario Lucia has gone from promising prospect to potential first rounder while putting together an impressive season. He is almost universally rated the top-ranked Minnesota high school prospect. In fact, many think he has surpassed Seth Ambroz as the top overall draft-eligible player from the North Star State. HockeyProspect.com's concerns with Ambroz's skating coupled with Lucia's productivity have led to the change as far as our rankings go. Lucia spent time with the United States National Team Development Program in November where he posted three goals in seven games en route to winning the Four Nations Cup in Sweden. Upon rejoining his high school team, the Wayzata Trojans, Lucia piled up points all season long.

With his 6-foot-2, 185-pound frame, Lucia already has ideal NHL frame. While he certainly needs to get bigger and stronger, Lucia wins battles pretty frequently. He also has a top-notch hockey IQ and sees the ice extremely well. That is expected when you're the son of a coach. Lucia's father, Don Lucia, is the bench boss for the University of Minnesota. While his body and hockey sense are quality attributes, Mario's skills are what had our scouts drooling. Lucia has a smooth and powerful skating stride. Despite his size, his first few steps are extremely quick. Lucia doesn't need much time to get to top speed. His hands are quick and very soft, he can score goals. Lucia has a blistering shot that is hard and accurate. His release is among the best in the draft.

Lucia's immediate future is undetermined at this point, but a few things are very clear. He will need to get much stronger and use his size to his advantage more frequently. He can be a bit soft at times right now and relies a lot on his exceptional skill set. But that shouldn't be too much of a deterrent to teams looking for a potential top-six forward. Lucia has a lot of time to round out his game.

Rickard Rakell

Right Wing – Plymouth Whalers (OHL)
Born May 5 1993 - Sollentuna, Sweden
Height 6.00 - Weight 191 - Shoots R

ROUND TWO #51

Games	Goals	Assists	Points	PIMS	+/-
49	19	24	43	12	+14

Rickard Rakell was selected 41st overall by the Plymouth Whalers in the 2010 CHL Import Draft. Rickard came out of the AIK program in Sweden, where he even got to play on their U20 team with his brother Robin for part of the season last year. Rakell chose to make the jump to the CHL, and it has proven to be a positive one with his participation in the CHL Top Prospects game. However, an injury affected the end of his season. He was only able to played in 1 playoff game; a game where he didn't see more than a few shifts.

Although technically listed as a winger, Rakell has spent most of his time at Center. If you were to talk to his head coach, Mike Velluci, he might tell you that the Whalers only had one real center on the team (Heard). Rickard is very strong on the forecheck, doesn't take very many shifts off and prides himself in his strong two-way ability.

Rakell is particularly effective when on the penalty kill. Has good hands and controls the puck well. He works hard along walls and protects the puck well using his body and feet to keep the puck in his possession. Rickard posted some decent numbers in his rookie OHL season with 19 goals and 24 assists in just 49 games. His injury suffered late in the season may have cost him scoring 25 goals as a rookie.

When trying to determine where to rank Rakell for the upcoming draft we focused on where we project him to play if he cracks an NHL lineup some day. We don't see top 6 scoring ability. In fact we don't think he is close as far as scoring and NHL shooting ability. Rakell showed nicely at the World Juniors in Buffalo by banging players around and playing a workmanlike game with a high motor running non-stop.

Seth Ambroz

Forward– Omaha Lancers (USHL)
Born Apr 1 1993 - New Prague, MN
Height 6.02 - Weight 211 - Shoots R

Games	Goals	Assists	Points	PIMS	+/-
56	24	22	46	89	NA

Omaha Lancer Seth Ambroz continues to play well in the USHL. He is one of the best forwards to come through the USHL in the past ten years.

Ambroz's biggest weakness is, without a doubt his skating. Transitioning from the offensive zone to backchecking is average, and he needs quite a few strides to get up to full speed. This puts him behind the play at times. Ambroz is strong on his skates. If he can improve on his skating while in the NCAA, Ambroz's value as a prospect will skyrocket.

The offensive zone is where Ambroz really shines. His wrist shot has incredible accuracy and power. He is a great passer as well. His passes are tape-to-tape ninety percent of the time. His scoring touch and his ability to score from pretty much anywhere in the offensive zone with his booming shot is what makes Ambroz a very special prospect. He is always ready and willing to crash the net and pay the price in front to get goals.

Ambroz has great hockey IQ. He has incredible vision that sets up Omaha's prolific power play, seeing passing lanes well before they develop, and that's what has lead to his statistical success throughout the years in the USHL. Ambroz also has improved a lot on his discipline this year compared to last, not taking as many dumb penalties and playing a clean and efficient game on the ice.

He is just as at home in the defensive zone as on the attack. He can block shots, clear the zone on the penalty kill, etc. He's one of the best back checkers in the USHL and his overall defensive abilities really help his draft value.

Joel Edmundson

Defense– Moose Jaw Warriors (WHL)
Born Jun 28 1993 - Brandon, MAN
Height 6.04 - Weight 191 - Shoots L

ROUND TWO #53

Games	Goals	Assists	Points	PIMS	+/-
71	2	18	20	95	+3

Joel Edmundson was a player who was off the radar a little bit until around midseason when he really improved his game. He became a key player on the Moose Jaw blueline as a rookie. Joel was drafted in the 6th Round of the 2008 WHL Bantam Draft by Moose Jaw. The Brandon, Manitoba native spent last season with the Brandon Wheat Kings AAA program, playing Midget hockey in Manitoba, putting up close to a point per game. Once the adjustment was made to the WHL he started to show off his potential at both ends of the ice.

Joel has tremendous size, and was actually recently measured at just between 6'4 and 6'5, and it isn't out of the question for him to get close to Tyler Myers territory. Joel still has a little bit work to do with his skating, but has shown visible improvement, and still has plenty of time to improve. He is a giant on the blueline, physical, has a big mean streak, and will finish his checks with authority as often as possible.

Edmundson has decent positioning in the defensive zone, and is a tough player to get inside on in front of the net. He is effective along the boards, but having big players on his blueline such as McIlrath, Ehrhart and McFaull help wear down the opposition, which doesn't hurt his cause. Joel has a good point shot, however he doesn't score a ton of goals. Evidence of this is in his statistics. However he is able to create offense with it, and his puck movement is solid thus seeing him rewarded with some power play time. Edmundson has the ability to drop the gloves as well, and did very well in one of the best fights I've seen all year against fellow draft eligible prospect Duncan Siemens.

With Edmundson improving at the rate he has been during this season, he has some unknown upside going into the draft. He has a lot of value basically with his size, and two-way play, but has proven to play fairly strong offensive, and as he gets his second full WHL season in, we could see his offense start to really show through.

Colin Jacobs

Center– Seattle Thunderbirds (WHL)
Born Jan 20 1993 - Coppell, TX
Height 6.01 - Weight 197 - Shoots R

Games	Goals	Assists	Points	PIMS	+/-
68	22	22	44	69	-20

The Seattle Thunderbirds did a very impressive job of finding hidden gems in the mid rounds of the 2008 WHL Bantam Draft. Possibly their best pick-up was finding Colin Jacobs still sitting there in the 4th round. Colin is a player who we consider the best of the five Seattle Thunderbirds ranked for this year's NHL Entry Draft.

Jacobs did not have a great top prospects game, which may affect his draft stock with some teams, but he has shown enough in league play down the stretch for us to be confident in having a positive opinion of him going into the draft.

Colin plays like a typical power forward. He has great size and uses it regularly both throwing hits, and battling in the corner, and winning many of those battles. Jacobs can take the puck and drive hard to the net. He has the strength to fight off checks en route to the net and in search of a scoring chance. Jacobs has a decent release on his shot, and has some good hands. Jacobs moves the puck well without much time to make a choice, but at times made some questionable decisions, which causes us to occasionally question his hockey sense.

Despite his size Jacobs tends to shy away from fighting, and has not fared well when choosing to drop the gloves, which we found surprising considering the size he possesses, and his effectiveness in the corners and along the boards. Jacobs will need to continue to add muscle, as he will need to stand up for himself at times when playing the style of game that he puts forward. There is some upside to his offensive skill, but it's tough to gauge at this point if Jacobs has 2nd or 3rd line potential at the NHL level. He could go as early as 2nd round if a team feels that his upside is in the top-six forward range.

Joseph Cramarossa

Center– Mississauga Majors (OHL)
Born Oct 26 1992 - Markham, ONT
Height 6.01 - Weight 188 - Shoots L

ROUND TWO #55

Games	Goals	Assists	Points	PIMS	+/-
59	12	20	32	101	+22

Joseph Cramarossa was selected in the 3rd round of the 2008 OHL Priority Selection by the Mississauga St. Michael's Majors. He graduated out of the Markham Majors' program to the OHL along with Andrew Crescenzi and J.P. Labardo. Cramarossa played for the Markham Waxers in the OJHL for one season, than made the jump to St. Michael's last season. He played in a fairly limited role, but was still able to produce, stir the pot a little, and show off his work ethic. It wasn't until this season where Joseph started to really make an impact, and forced observers of the Majors team to take notice. Joseph isn't the kind of player you go to the game to see, but he is the kind of player to leave an impression on you by the time the game is over.

Cramarossa is a player who leads by example, and puts out an outstanding work ethic every shift he takes. Joseph has shown to have a good hockey IQ and understands the game very well, despite not getting a great deal of ice time. Cramarossa is at his best when he's in the corners, or battling along the boards. He wins a large amount of battles, but what separates him from the common "grinder" is that he has the awareness and the vision to know what to do with the puck after he wins the battle. He can make both difficult passes, and unleash a solid shot, and has shown some good moves 1 on 1 with goaltenders. This takes Cramarossa from being a low risk, 3rd line energy type player, and adds an element of being a potential top 6 NHL forward. When given a bigger role, Joseph might just show off some intriguing offensive point producing skills. His younger brother, a 1996 birth is blessed with great offensive talent, so there is scoring skill in the bloodlines.

In addition to all of this, Joseph is an excellent penalty killer. To be looked to as a key player on the PK on a veteran team is very impressive. Cramarossa takes the same pride in battling in the offensive zone, and uses it in his own end. He will also dive in front of shots and block them without hesitation. We would like to see Cramarossa become a bit mentally stronger dealing with adversity. Sometimes things seem to knock him off his game for a few shifts. This should improve with maturity though. Cramarossa is a low risk prospect with upside. Every time we've seen him play this season, we've left the game more impressed with his work ethic and potential.

Brenden Kichton

Defense – Spokane Chiefs (WHL)
Born Jun 18 1992 - Spruce Grove, ALTA
Height 5.11 - Weight 185 - Shoots L

Games	Goals	Assists	Points	PIMS	+/-
64	23	58	81	31	+55

After not being selected in last year's entry draft, Brenden Kichton has blossomed into one of the elite puck moving defensemen in the Western Hockey League. Kichton came into the 2010/11 campaign a much stronger and more developed player than the year before, partially due to having a strong off-season workout. He also found more opportunity this season playing on the Chiefs top defensive pairing, alongside Ottawa Senators prospect Jared Cowen. The 18 year old blue-liner went from scoring 19 points in 2009/10, to scoring an outstanding 23 goals and 81 points in 2010/11. Kichton was rewarded for his breakout season by being named to the Western Conference's second All-Star team.

Kichton's success can be attributed to his strong hockey sense. He has a phenomenal skill level at reading players and positioning himself into the offensive and defensive zones. Kichton's smooth skating abilities make it easy for him to lead offensive rushes. His major claim to fame has been his success quarterbacking the Chiefs power-play. Kichton often sets up teammates with crisp smooth passes, 33 of Kichton's 58 assists came on the power-play. Shooting wise, Kichton usually decides to take wrist shots due to not having an overly strong slap shot. The biggest question on Kichton is how much does playing on a strong Chiefs team factor into his offensive statistics.

Kichton's exceptional offensive play often overshadows his strong defensive play. He's continued to be a reliable defensive player, maintaining a plus-55 throughout the 2010/11 season. He often plays a vital role on the penalty-kill, using his strong active stick. Despite having a 5-foot-11, 185 pound frame, Kichton isn't afraid of physical play. However, he's had trouble in puck battles with some of the bigger and stronger opponents.

Tyler Wotherspoon

Defense – Portland (WHL)
Born Mar 12 1993 - Surrey, BC
Height 6.01 - Weight 203 - Shoots L

Games	Goals	Assists	Points	PIMS	+/-
64	2	10	12	73	0

Wotherspoon was selected in the 2nd round of the 2008 WHL Bantam Draft. He hasn't had a ton of exposure until this year, when he really started to show what he could do. Only playing 47 games going into this season, Tyler used his great size to get noticed, as he became a player that no one wanted to play against.

Wotherspoon is a very physical player, and is particularly tough along the boards and in the corners. He seems to understand his role fairly well and embraces it as he punishes opposing forwards, and uses his NHL ready size to clear out the front of his own net. With the puck he will make a smart first pass, and high percentage plays in terms of clearing out the zone.

Offensively, on the surface there doesn't appear to be a ton of upside; however, he moves the puck very effectively, and can move the puck under pressure respectably well. The biggest concern for Wotherspoon is his skating. Because he is not a great skater, but a defensive first player, he will come off the offensive line too early and will be out by the red line when he could be holding the line. Conversely, when holding the line Wotherspoon needs to make good reads. If the opposition can chip pucks by him, Wotherspoon struggles to catch up. Working on his first few steps, then improving the top speed will be the biggest task for Wotherspoon, as he already has the NHL size, and the knowledge to uses it appropriately, but skating improvements will be the biggest key in his success going forward.

David Musil

Defense – Vancouver Giants (WHL)
Born Apr 9 1993 - Delta, BC
Height 6.03 - Weight 198 - Shoots L

Games	Goals	Assists	Points	PIMS	+/-
62	6	19	25	83	0

Musil was born in Canada, however is of Czech heritage, and represents them internationally. David's father Frank played 14 seasons in the NHL, and calls recently retired Bobby Holik his uncle, so David has the bloodlines going for him. He has certainly inherited his father's size.

David's hometown is located only 30 minutes outside Vancouver so he likely knew the area well, and it played a role in him being moved from the Kootenay Ice to the Vancouver Giants during the summer of 2009 in exchange for two draft picks.

David is a physical player who uses his size to hit players hard; however, we have noticed him losing an alarming amount of battles along the boards and in the corners. His defensive positioning is solid, and has done well in fights but we'd like to see him get a little more upper body strength and add to his frame a little more. Musil has very respectable skating abilities for someone his size, and has shown some solid two way potential.

Musil has a big point shot and unloads it at will. He has done respectably well on the power play. He moves the puck effectively; however, he does make a few mistakes. He has helped Vancouver on the power play but the recurring theme with David is that he keeps leaving us wanting more out of him.

Ultimately David will still have a shot at the first round; however, we see him landing somewhere in the 2nd. Musil is a tough player to project because he has a great package of talent, and the bloodlines to go with it, but will get picked based on how good he could be, rather than what he has accomplished thus far. There is still a great deal of potential surrounding David Musil, and we look forward to seeing if he can start reaching his projected potential.

Jordon Binnington

Goalie – Owen Sound (OHL)
Born Jul 11 1993 - Richmond Hill, ONT
Height 6.01 - Weight 156 - Catches L

Games	Wins	Losses	G.A.A	Save %	SO
46	27	12	3.05	.899	1

Binnington is a former second round pick in the OHL Priority Selection and was featured in the HockeyProspect.com 2011 Prospect Preview. He played for one of the top OHL teams this season in Owen Sound. He played in the CHL Top Prospects game and overall has improved his draft stock this season. Binnington says the best piece of advice he ever received was to keep battling, and prides himself on his technique and reflexes. He loves to watch Marc-Andre Fleury play and tries to model his game after the former #1 overall pick.

Binnington got a chance to do something that many other goalies in their draft year don't get to do. He got to play. Owen Sound's starter Scott Stacjer suffered an injury that knocked him out of action until the first round of the playoffs. Binnington had the ball handed to him and did a very good job of running with it. Although he lost his starting job in the playoffs, he did start the first round series versus the London Knights and had some success. It became a bit of a musical goalies situation in the playoffs with three goalies sharing time. Some would argue that Jordan got a bit of a raw deal, but such is life for goaltenders.

Binnington is a tall lanky kid with a very slight build. His father is just huge, so that might suggest that he is not done growing and filling out just yet, if you subscribe to that sort of thinking. Jordan moves very well in his net, and tracks the puck around the zone. He anticipates the play pretty well and shows good reflexes. He is very quick post to post and does not show any glaring weakness. He covers the bottom of the net well and has good gloves. Our knock on Binnington would probably be lapses in concentration. Going back to his Vaughan Kings days and with the Attack, he can be prone to some soft goals. We expect this to improve with maturity. Jordan is a top goalie prospect in 2011 and our top draft eligible goalie from the OHL.

David Honzik

Goalie – Victoriaville Tigres (QMJHL)
Born Aug 9 1993 -Tabor, CZE
Height 6.02 - Weight 209 - Catches L

HOCKEYPROSPECT.COM

ROUND TWO #60

Games	Wins	Losses	G.A.A	Save %	SO
36	17	12	3.54	.884	1

The European goalie was in his rookie season this year in North American hockey and he took a good deal of time adapting to his new environment. Honzik was the second goalie behind veteran Antonio Mastropietro. But as the 19 year old Mastropietro became inconsistent at the end of the season, the youngster took over with solid performances and was the number one goalie for the remainder of the season and in the playoffs.

There is good size here with the Czech Republic native. We like that he is calm and cool in front of his net. He has good lateral movement and good reflexes to make very quick leg saves. We like his quickness with the pads and he has a really good glove hand. The biggest problem with the young goalie is consistency. When Honzik is in the zone, he makes key save, after key save, but that's not something he has been able to do every night. He's a big guy, so the puck should hit him if he challenges shooters, but he needs to be aggressive. Honzik seems be only be aggressive if he is in his zone. He was the best goalie in the playoffs in the Q this year, at least while his team was involved anyway. He is very athletic; he makes a lot of spectacular saves with incredible flexibility. We love the way he competes every night and never gives up on a play. He is very good at finding the puck in traffic and making saves with bodies in front of him.

Honzik needs to work on his mental toughness. He needs to be as good in a 16 shot game as in a 45 shot game. He also needs to work on rebound control and redirecting them into the corners.

Tobias Rieder

Right Wing – Kitchener Rangers
Born Jan 10, 1993 - Landshut, Germany
Height 5.10 - Weight 169 - Shoots L

HOCKEYPROSPECT.COM

DRAFT GUIDE' 11

Games	Goals	Assists	Points	PIMS	+/-
65	23	26	49	35	+9

Tobias Rieder was selected 5th overall in the 2010 CHL Import Draft. The Kitchener Rangers were eventually able to convince Rieder to come to the OHL after consideration of staying in Germany to play professionally. Tobias is no stranger to goal scoring, as he put up 113 goals in only 34 games played at the age of 14 and 15 in the German under 16 league. He was then moved up to the U18 league at the age of 15, where he promptly became the 2nd leading scorer in the league. Rieder took very little time to adjust to North American hockey putting up a goal in each of his first two games, the second of which was a huge goal as it was the turning point in the hockey game. He had a total of 5 points in those 2 games.

Tobias Rieder is a great skater, and uses this talent to rush the puck, and also be tenacious on the puck carrier as a fore-checker. Rieder also works very hard in the defensive zone, and is a capable player along the boards due to his relentless pressure. He feeds off making opposing players make mistakes. Rieder always seems to start the game very strong, and usually is a high-lighted player during the 3rd period. However, there are times as the game moves along (usually end of the 1st, or middle of the 2nd) where Rieder has shown a tendency to take a few shifts off. This is one of the few knocks on his game. Rieder is dangerous whenever he touches the puck in the offensive zone due to an absolute laser of a wrist shot, but also displays a respectably strong slap shot. Rieder is also capable of creating offense for his teammates in the offensive zone. However, his positioning without the puck when his team is in possession still raises some question marks.

Overall Rieder has some great potential and Top 6 forward skills at the highest level, but also does a lot of the little things that would make him a valuable bottom 6 player. However, there are some flaws revolving around some hockey sense issues such as positioning and consistency that may raise questions in some NHL GM's.

Phillip Danault

Left Wing – Victoriaville Tigre (QMJHL)
Born Feb 24 1993 - Victoriaville, PQ
Height 5.11 – Weight - 170 - Shoots L

Games	Goals	Assists	Points	PIMS	+/-
64	23	44	67	59	+17

At the age of 17, Danault is already the captain of a very offensive squad in Victoriaville. He is a leader on and off the ice at a young age and his point production kept getting better as the season went on. The speedy young gun can play in every situation on the ice and he'll do whatever it takes to get a win for his team.

The main strength of Philip Danault is his speed. He can make a lot of defensemen look bad by going wide on them and then driving to the net. He plays a pretty simple game for a skilled guy. He anticipates plays very well and he creates most of his scoring chances from hard work and speed. He can create beautiful plays off the rush as he has good vision and always plays with his head up. He has really good strength overall in his body to win battles against bigger and older players. He never stops working, no matter what the scoreboard says.

Danault is a terrific penalty killer. He plays an aggressive game and he's tough to handle for defenseman because he comes at them very quickly. Danault is a good 2-way player and coaches will want him on the ice in all situations. He leads by example and you definitely want him on your team. Danault is a team first guy who would seem to be a born leader.

Phillip needs to polish some parts of his game. His shot needs to get better and be more accurate. He handles the puck pretty well but he needs to use that more during game situations. Some players just try to keep it too simple sometimes and in some games. We feel Danault could create a lot more if he was more confident in his ability. He can be too aggressive at times, taking bad penalties. He can get his team in trouble sometimes by being out of position in the D zone. It usually happens when the play gets intense; he can put too much intensity in his own play. Our concern with Danault is where does he fit in the NHL? Not having elite skills and being slightly smallish frame wise is always a red flag for NHL teams when drafting.

Andrew Fritsch

Right Wing – Owen Sound Attack
Born Mar 24 1993 - Brantford, ONT
Height 6.00 - Weight 187 - Shoots R

HOCKEYPROSPECT.COM

DRAFT GUIDE' 11

Games	Goals	Assists	Points	PIMS	+/-
60	28	35	63	18	+19

The Niagara Ice Dogs selected Andrew Fritsch in the 3rd round, in what was an excellent draft for Niagara, selecting fellow top 2011 NHL Entry Draft prospects Lucas Lessio and Dougie Hamilton in the two previous rounds. Fritsch came out of the Brantford 99'ers AAA program. Fritsch made the Ice Dogs as a 16 year old and put up a respectable 11 goals in his rookie season. In addition to this, Fritsch became a fan favorite with his energetic play.

Although Owen Sound's stars Joey Hishon and Garrett Wilson get a lot of the attention for the Attack's offensive output, Andrew Fritsch has quietly put up very solid numbers. Fritsch started out the year playing on the 2nd and 3rd lines where he was an important part of creating offense for his line. It's his time on the 1st line that is really showing off how dangerous Fritsch can be when he's given a little space.

Fritsch shows off good hockey sense, and his positioning is very solid in all areas of the ice. Fritsch has decent skating abilities, and uses them to create offense while on the Attack in the opposing team's zone. Fritch has spent a huge chunk of the playoffs on the sideline witch hurts his development. There is no substitute for experience gained in the playoffs, especially with the long run the Attack have made this season.

Our overall take on Fritsch is that he is a highly skilled player with great scoring ability. Our knock on him is that he can play too soft. We dropped him in our rankings based on his lack of 'want to' when it comes to hunting down pucks in the dirty areas. Both he and teammate, Jarrod Maidens, (2012) both need to show more willingness to win races to lose pucks. No more pulling the chute. Andrew will raise his game to the next level if he can play a more gritty game.

Scott Harrington

Defense – London Knights (OHL)
Born Mar 10 1993 - Kingston, ONT
Height 6.01 - Weight 200 - Shoots L

Games	Goals	Assists	Points	PIMS	+/-
67	6	16	22	51	-14

Scott Harrington was selected 19th overall in the 2009 OHL Priority Selection by the London Knights. He made a trip to the RBC Cup with the Junior 'A' Kingston Voyageurs as a call-up after his Minor Midget season came to an end. Harrington took his time developing and focused on the defensive part of his game in year one., By the end of the year he developed into a top 4 defenseman for the Knights.

This year Harrington has spent most of his time on the top pairing. He was learning from the overage defenseman Michael D'Orazio until D'Orazio was moved at the trade deadline to Mississauga. Harrington has since continued to gain responsibility on the Knights blueline. Harrington is getting key minutes in all game situations and is playing well over 20 minutes per game.

Harrington plays a two-way game, but leans more towards the defensive side of the game. He is very mature for his age. Harrington commonly makes a few great defensive plays per game, and is generally very reliable on the defensive side of play. His positioning appeared to improve throughout the season.

Harrington makes the smart first pass out of his own zone a high percentage of the time. A decent skater, and has always shown some offensive potential in his game, but still has yet to produce at the rate expected at this point in his career. He displays a solid slap shot from the point, but is also is willing to move in and release a wrist shot if the opposition gives him space. Harrington has a big frame, and handles physical play well; however, doesn't willingly engage nearly enough for his size. Harrington will rush the puck up the ice; however, he generally does not look all that comfortable when doing so. One of the biggest concerns for Harrington is, despite making a lot of great defensive plays, he has known to make the occasional major mental error, which directly results in a scoring chance or a goal.

Brandon Francisco

Left Wing – Sarnia Sting (OHL)
Born Feb 11 1993 - Bradford, ONT
Height 5.10 - Weight 175 - Shoots L

Games	Goals	Assists	Points	PIMS	+/-
61	14	16	30	6	-25

Brandon Francisco was selected in the 3rd round on the 2009 OHL Priority Selection by the Sarnia Sting. Francisco fell from 1st round projections due to a verbal commitment to Maine University. Brandon played for a powerhouse York-Simcoe Express team which also produced Daniel Catenacci and Ryan Murphy the same year. Francisco eventually made the decision to join the Sarnia Sting of the OHL, but got off to a slow start in his rookie season, despite making the team as a 16 year old out of camp. The second half of the season saw a much more successful Francisco, as he was the 2nd highest scoring rookie from the post-Christmas break through to the end of the season. Some scouts may still not realize that Brandon Francisco is eligible for this year's draft, due to a misprint. This misprint has been since been fixed.

Francisco's skill is highlighted by his speed and skating ability. Francisco can accelerate quickly, and he has a top speed that can allow him to break away. Francisco was a player who would sometimes try to do too much with the puck. He has improved greatly in this area since then and utilizes his line mates fairly effectively. Francisco has a quick release on his shot, and although he hasn't put up a ton of goals, 3 or 4 of his goals have been highlight reel material. Francisco has developed a reputation for great discipline as he only has 9 minor penalties in 2 seasons. Francisco has also added muscle to his frame.

Francisco has shown at times that he will take a big hit in order to make a play that directly results in a scoring chance. Brandon's defensive play has been a work in progress. He has been improving; however, outside of his size issues, consistency has been his greatest battle. On Francisco's good days, he has good defensive coverage, keeps an active stick in the passing lane, and is the first forward in defensive positioning on his line. However, on bad days, defensive coverage and general work ethic are very sparse, and he does not display the offensive creativity he usually shows. If he can play a stronger overall game on a consistent basis, he has a good chance of becoming a more legitimate NHL prospect.

Zach Bell

Defense – Brampton Battalion (OHL)
Born Feb 13 1993 - Brampton, ONT
Height 6.02 - Weight 211 - Shoots R

HOCKEYPROSPECT.COM

DRAFT GUIDE '11

Games	Goals	Assists	Points	PIMS	+/-
63	3	9	12	86	-2

Zach Bell was a 4th round pick of the Battalion in the 2009 OHL Draft. Bell made the team and played in 46 games as a rookie. The team was stacked with veteran defenseman so getting icetime was a chore. Fast forward to this season and after a slow start, Bell has elevated himself to the top pairing. His minutes have increased as the season has progressed.

Bell is a big tough defenseman who sometimes looks too often for the big hit. He has improved in this regard though. HP's Director of Scouting, Mark Edwards, had this to say about Bell. "Bell has come miles since I first saw him in midget. His skating has always been a little ugly to watch, but he is lightning fast in a straight line. Where Zach has improved, is in his mobility. He is by no means a pretty skater but he has really learned to play so much smarter and within himself. His puck moving ability has improved and is very good. His offensive skills are under-rated. Bell is not afraid to drop the gloves and has fared ok when he has had the occasional fight."

Bell has a great catch and release at the offensive blueline and does a good job getting his pucks through. His wrist shot is hard. He sometimes lets it fly a bit high but he is still pretty accurate. His biggest improvement has come in his own zone. Bell is making fewer mistakes in coverage and is winning the majority of physical battles along the wall. His outlet passes were fantastic from about game 25 onward. He made excellent decisions with the puck and made accurate passes to spring his forwards on the breakout. He showed excellent poise controlling the puck while he scanned his options. He was buying himself time and showed great communication skills on the ice. He took charge as the season has progressed and did well communicating the right play with his partner and goaltender.

Bell just needs to improve some more on letting the hits come to him. He was probably trying to show scouts his physical play and chased too many hits. He also needs to get up ice a bit quicker and more consistently. Sometimes he gets caught watching forwards on the rush and forgets to join the attack. Bell has made some impressive rushes this season in which he showed his speed and underrated offensive talent. Bell has NHL bloodlines as his birth father is former NHL'er Bruce Bell.

Vincent Trocheck

Center- Saginaw Spirit (OHL)
Born Jul 11 1993 - Pittsburgh, PA
Height 5.10 - Weight 184 - Shoots R

HOCKEYPROSPECT.COM

DRAFT GUIDE' 11

Games	Goals	Assists	Points	PIMS	+/-
68	26	36	62	60	+14

Vincent Trocheck was drafted out of the Detroit Little Ceasars program, and selected 24th overall by the Saginaw Spirit in the 2009 OHL Priority Selection. The Pittsburgh native made the Spirit as a 16 year old. He had a very respectable rookie season and was an impressive 2nd in team scoring for the Spirit during the 2010 playoffs. Vincent's role has expanded with the team this season, as he quietly put up good numbers yet again.

Trocheck is a player who is considered a safe pick based on his game. Trocheck is very solid in all three zones, and prides himself on his hard work in the defensive zone. Trocheck is less dynamic than other small forwards such as Catenacci and Khokhlachev, but he see's himself ranked in the same general area due to his defensive game, and his great hockey sense. Vincent has some elusive moves and creates offense very effectively. We have seen a lack of high end acceleration and speed; this hinders some of his upside.

Despite possessing average skating attributes, Trocheck has the hands and intelligence to anticipate plays, and creates offense for both himself and his team. Trocheck is not afraid to hit and seems to finish his checks on a fairly regular basis. Vincent sees himself regularly on the penalty kill with fellow prospect Brandon Saad. He has been very effective getting his stick in passing lanes, and even creating offense for himself and his PK partner. Part of what makes him such a strong penalty killer is his great face-off capabilities. This was highlighted in the OHL Coaches Poll which voted Trocheck the second best in the face-off circle among Western Conference players.

Ultimately Vincent Trocheck is a solid prospect, who is an effective two-way forward. If he can improve in his skating and combine that with his creativity and intelligence, Trocheck may have the potential to play in a second line role in the NHL.

67

Alex Lepkowski

Defense – Barrie Colts (OHL)
Born Apr 8 1993 - West Seneca, NY
Height 6.03 - Weight 216 - Shoots L

HOCKEYPROSPECT.COM

DRAFT GUIDE' 11

Games	Goals	Assists	Points	PIMS	+/-
39	0	6	6	75	-3

Alex Lepkowski, a defenseman from the state of New York, was drafted out of St. Francis High School in the 4th round of the 2009 OHL Priority Selection by the Saginaw Spirit. Alex chose to report to the Spirit, and began his OHL career making Saginaw right out of camp as a 16 year old. Although he received limited ice time, Lepkowski showed that he had some good potential. Alex did get some exposure this season for Saginaw. The problem he ran into was the deep blueline, on a contending team. Lepkowski was eventually dealt to the rebuilding Barrie Colts as a key part of the deal that sent Dalton Prout to Saginaw.

Lepkowski is a huge, physical defenseman, who takes care of his own zone, and likes to play physical. We were impressed with his body positioning in 1 on 1 battles, as well as odd man rushes and overall positioning in the defensive zone. Lepkowski is always thinking defense and will generally retreat at the first sign of trouble to maintain that positioning.

Lepkowski is very limited offensively, and has actually not scored yet in his OHL career. Alex plays physical, and has the ability to punish the opposition, He will at times throw a dirty hit causing his team to go shorthanded. He has been known to end up in a fight the odd time as well. Although Lepkowski has held his own for the most part, fighting hasn't been one of his strong areas. On one occasion, he appeared to have lingering effects which affected his playing time for the remainder of the season.

We see Lepkowski as a safe defensive player. He should make a good option later on in this draft, as he possesses great size, good positional play, effective handling of 1 on 1 situations, and physicality. If he can clean up his physical play, and be a physical presence without going over the line too often, Lepkowski could turn into a solid shutdown defender at both the OHL level, and beyond.

68

Anthony Camara

Left Wing - Saginaw (OHL)
Born Sep 4 1993 - Toronto, ONT
Height 6.00 - Weight 194 - Shoots R

HOCKEYPROSPECT.COM

DRAFT GUIDE' 11

Games	Goals	Assists	Points	PIMS	+/-
64	8	9	17	132	-9

Anthony Camara was Saginaw's 1st round pick in the 2009 OHL Priority Selection, going 15th overall. Camara came out of a Mississauga Senators program which also produced fellow prospects Frank Palazzese, Alex Basso, and also Kitchener Ranger defenceman, Ben Fanelli. Camara came into camp as a 16 year old and played himself into a roster spot. Although not gaining a lot of ice time, Camara would fight more than any other 1993 born player in his rookie season.

Camara is highlighted by his strength and physicality. Anthony likes to play on the edge. He has gone over it a few times, and occasionally hasn't stopped when a player has been in a vulnerable position. Despite that, he has established himself as one of the more devastating physical players in the league, at only 17 years old. Evidence of this appears in the OHL Coaches poll where he was overwhelmingly voted as the "Best Body Checker" in the Western Conference.

Beyond his physical play, Camara is a decent skater, which he has used in combination with his size to protect the puck well. He has shown the ability to frustrate opposing players, forcing them to take penalties. Camara was used before the trade deadline on the power play, where he proved to frustrate opposing defenders as he was constantly moving around down low, cutting off goaltenders vision, then moving into open areas giving him the opportunity to score. Camara also possesses a decent shot when given the opportunity to use it.

HP scout Ryan Yessie elaborates on Camara: "Anthony has been an intriguing prospect right from the start. He's a guy who has shown the ability to do a little bit of everything, but never too much of anything. He understands his limitations, and plays within them. Camara will never be an elite goal scorer, but he has some interesting offensive upside. He plays a physical game and is player who understands his role. He will stand up for his teammates without hesitation."

Brett Findlay

Left Wing – Soo Greyhounds (OHL)
Born Oct 13 1992 - Echo Bay, ONT
Height 6.00 - Weight 160 - Shoots L

Games	Goals	Assists	Points	PIMS	+/-
57	20	24	44	31	-3

The fact that Findlay is even playing hockey these days, let alone at the OHL level is quite amazing. In 2007, Findlay broke the fibula and tibia bones in one of his legs in an all-terrain-vehicle accident that required major surgery. Skating is in the gene pool in the Findlay family. His older sister Terra is a world class skater and mom is a skating instructor who has worked for the Greyhounds.

The skinny, but speedy winger, who missed the first 11 games of his first season with a fractured wrist, put up some nice numbers for Sault Ste. Marie this season, averaging nearly a point per game. He has nice net drive, can play on the power play, and if he can get stronger, he could really turn out to be a very good prospect.

Brett has come a long way this season. He struggled with the defensive side of his game early on in his rookie campaign. He changed that in the second half of the season. Although he is far from a defensive specialist, he showed the ability to make great strides in defensive coverage, fore-checking and winning more 1 on 1 battles. He made far less mistakes getting caught on the wrong side of the puck.

The offensive side of Brett's game is quite impressive. With this season being both his rookie season and his NHL darft year as a late 1992 birthdate, Findlay has done a nice job of impressing scouts. Findlay sees the ice well and has become a better decision maker with the puck in all three zones. Brett was making far too many unforced turnovers early in the season. Findlay really shines in the skating category. This kid can really fly and as the season progressed, he has learned to better utilize his speed as a weapon.

Joachim Nermark

C/LW – Linköping (SWE)
Born May 12 1993 - Sunne, SWE
Height 6.01 - Weight 190 - Shoots L

HOCKEYPROSPECTION.COM

DRAFT GUIDE' 11

Games	Goals	Assists	Points	PIMS	+/-
37	8	18	26	16	NA

Some players just have a sense of where to be on the ice. Swedish center Joachim Nermark is one of those players. His hockey sense and ability to recognize plays is his best asset, but the 6-foot-1, 190-pounder has terrific skills as well. Nermark has good size and protects the puck well in the offensive zone. He is a responsible player at both ends of the rink. He has quickly moved up the junior ranks in Sweden and has even seen time at the Swedish Elite League level this season.

Excellent skating is one of Nermark's best traits. He has a quick first few steps and good top-end speed. Nermark has an elite set of hands to go along with his above-average size and skating ability. He is a creative player that is equally adept as a shooter or a passer. As seen by his five goal, six assist performance at the Ivan Hlinka Tournament, Nermark can play under pressure. He is able to find the quiet areas of the ice using his high hockey IQ. Even when he gets caught in traffic, Nermark's creativity and skill are enough to make a play. He should probably have better numbers with his skill level, but with more experience and confidence, the numbers will come.

A couple of seasons at Sweden's top professional level are probably in Nermark's future. He will not be a player that will be ready for the NHL right away, but he could blossom into a steady point producer in the future. Nermark should be a solid pick because of his size, speed, commitment and work ethic.

Alan Quine

Center – Peterborough Petes (OHL)
Born Feb 25 1993 - Ottawa, ONT
Height 5.11 - Weight 178 - Shoots L

HOCKEYPROSPECT.COM

DRAFT GUIDE' 11

Games	Goals	Assists	Points	PIMS	+/-
69	26	27	53	8	-36

Alan Quine was the 2nd overall pick in the 2009 OHL Priority Selection behind only Daniel Catenacci. Alan Quine graduated from the Toronto Jr. Canadiens program which also features fellow 2011 NHL Entry Draft prospects Tyler Biggs and Zach Bell. Alan had a respectable rookie season for the Kingston Frontenacs, and looked like a big part of their future; however, 17 games into this OHL season, Alan saw himself heading to Peterborough as a key part of a blockbuster deal which saw Boston Bruins prospect Ryan Spooner sent to Kingston. Quine was immediately inserted with fellow top prospect Matthew Puempel, up until Puempel's season ending hip injury. Once he settled in, Quine was consistently a key player for the Petes, at one point putting up 11 goals in 10 games. After Puempel was out of the line-up, Quine's production became fairly inconsistent, and all in all had he a rough end to the season.

Quine's talent in the face-off circle is at a high level. He is arguably one of the best available in the draft in this category. He won draws at an outstanding rate in the games we saw him this season. Quine is a smart player with high hockey IQ, and he is good in his positioning most of the time. Quine is a decent skater, and it's an area that will naturally get better as he improves the strength in his legs. Quine has got bigger and a stronger this year, but it's an area where he needs to continue to work hard. His lack of strength is a part of his game that can jump out at you in some games.

Quine is a player that can frustrate you at times. He sways too far in the 'pass first' direction too often for our liking. He sometimes has games where resembles Thomas Kaberle and it seems like he will never shoot. We would love to see him start shooting more often. Make no mistake, this kid is a goal scorer and is at the high end of the class as far as thinking the game. If Quine is a big draft day slider he could end up being an absolute steal for an NHL team somewhere down the road.

Mike Moffat

Defense– London Knights (OHL)
Born Jun 12 1993 - Waterloo, ONT
Height 6.01 - Weight 205 - Shoots L

HOCKEYPROSPECT.COM

DRAFT GUIDE' 11

Games	Goals	Assists	Points	PIMS	+/-
47	2	7	9	37	-6

Mike Moffat has taken a more difficult route to the OHL then most. The 1993 born defenseman played Midget AAA last season for the Waterloo Wolves and made the Knights as a free agent. The big defenseman posted some points last season and from our viewings this season in the OHL, this kid does not lack in the confidence department. He shows great poise when he takes off with the puck and has chosen his spots to rush well.

Moffat made the transition to the OHL look pretty easy. He has very good size. He was very good in his own zone. He won a good share of his one on one battles, winning along the walls and in front of the net. Moffat has shown good gap control both off the rush and playing his man tight in the neutral zone. His stick work has been good as well. He does a pretty good job of taking away lanes.

What jumped out at us right away in our first viewing of this player was his poise. He had not yet even played 5 OHL games and he seemed so calm and confident with the puck. Most players in his situation just get rid of the puck before they have time to make a big mistake. This was not the case for Mike Moffat. He played very loose, like as if he was out playing shinny with his buddies-not careless, just loose.

Moffat is one of our 'under the radar picks' this year. We think his upside is quite good. We don't see a big weakness in his game. Moffat has size, skating, poise, defensive awareness, offensive skills and smarts. We wish he got more ice time. We won't be shocked if he somehow finds his way to being drafted despite some limited playing time this season. Mike needs to get in slightly better shape heading into next year.

Alex Basso

Defense – Belleville Bulls (OHL)
Born Jun 15 1993 - Toronto, ONT
Height 5.11 - Weight 176 - Shoots

Games	Goals	Assists	Points	PIMS	+/-
57	5	16	21	36	-20

Alex Basso was one of the best selections made outside the top 75 of the OHL Priority Selection when the Belleville Bulls selected him late in the 4th round. Basso came from the Mississauga Senators program, and was teammates with fellow 2011 NHL Entry Draft prospects Anthony Camara, Ben Fanelli and Franky Palazzese. Basso made the Bulls out of camp as a 16 year old, and proceeded to have a fairly successful rookie season.

He is a decent skater who will rush the puck up the ice and is very elusive at doing so; however, also recognizes when to pass in this scenario. Alex will play physical despite his size, and has been seen standing up for himself and his teammates. Playing in Belleville Alex got a number of opportunities to show off his skills on the special teams. On the power play he was a very underrated contributor who was calm under pressure, and has a respectable shot from the point. On the penalty kill Basso was fairly reliable and seemed to make the right play with the puck in his own zone.

Basso doesn't do any one thing tremendously well, but doesn't really have any glaring weaknesses either. He is not a player we expect to be a huge game breaker, but rather a safe, reliable defenseman who understands the game, and can benefit his team without being a liability at the highest level. His positioning is solid, and it is actually when Belleville is at it's worst, that Basso really shows his true value. He is never too high and never too low, so he tends to be Belleville's best and most reliable defenseman, when they're going through a rough game, or rough series of games. Alex is very quietly showing his value, and is a defenseman we were consistently happy with.

Olivier Archambault

Left Wing– Val d'Or Foreurs (QMJHL)
Born Feb 16 1993 - Le Gardeur, PQ
Height 5.11 - Weight 170 - Shoots L

Games	Goals	Assists	Points	PIMS	+/-
65	20	33	53	28	-7

Olivier Archambault is one of the most talented young men with the puck in this draft along with Tomas Jurco.

This kid is pretty special. On the ice, he is a dangling machine; he is a flashy player but we wish sometimes he would a more simple game rather than the more high risk game he plays too often. He is very unpredictable with the puck and can dangle it in a phone booth. Olivier Archambault's great hands along with his great speed gives him tools to create a lot of time and space for himself in the offensive zone and thus allows him to create scoring opportunities.

With Olivier Archambault, NHL teams will need to accept the good with the bad. He is a young man that has elite-level talent with the puck, but his decision making can be pretty poor at times. He holds on the puck for too long and causes turnovers. He wants to be too fancy sometimes and can't seem to simplify his game. Archambault's use of teammates is pretty poor overall. We would like to see him get more aggressive along the boards because he is pretty strong for a sub- six foot kid.

In his own zone, his positioning is good and he knows where to be on the ice to cut down offensive chances, but his lack of physicality causes him to lose proper body positioning. In too many cases this results in lost 1 on 1 battles and needless puck possession for opposing teams. If Olivier stepped it up physically and made better decisions with the puck it would raise his draft stock with us in a big way. He has elite skill which makes his upside very high.

Olivier Archambault is so close yet so far from being an elite level prospect.

Myles Bell

Defense – Regina Pats (WHL)
Born Aug 13 1993 - Calgary, ALTA
Height 6.00 - Weight 214 - Shoots R

Games	Goals	Assists	Points	PIMS	+/-
68	14	31	45	86	-14

Myles Bell was selected 17th overall by the Regina Pats in the 2008 Bantam Draft. Myles played a number of games with the Pats as a 15 year old before playing a full season as a 16 year old. Myles played well enough in the first half of the season to join Canada Pacific in the U17 challenge. Bell did extremely well, posting 4 goals in 5 games, a number that matched his totals from his entire rookie season in the WHL. Myles has taken on a much bigger role with the Pats this season. He has produced very well offensively, and receives key minutes on the power play.

Myles has an outstanding point shot, and was able to bury 14 goals this season largely because of it. His slap shot already reaches numbers that some NHLers are unable to match. His wrist shot is pretty effective as well. In addition to this, Myles is a very effective puck mover in the offensive zone. He shows respectable mobility on the point during the powerplay. Bell is actually a decent skater for his size, and is capable at rushing the puck up the ice, as well as jumping into the rush undetected to help the team out offensively.

Defensively Bell has respectable positioning in his own zone, and stays with the play well. The biggest issue we had with Bell's game, is he doesn't use his size effectively enough and it was constantly frustrating seeing him pass up opportunities to throw his weight around.

Moving forward, Bell will likely need to hit the weight room to get stronger. He needs to become more willing to show his strength. We wonder about his fitness regime, as he appears to look a little sluggish later on in games. This might just be a need for conditioning improvement. Myles has a lot of upside, particularly on the power play, but he could turn into a solid all around defenseman.

Brent Benson

Center – Saskatoon Blades (WHL)
Born Apr 13 1993 - Weyburn, SASK
Height 5.11 - Weight 183 - Shoots L

Games	Goals	Assists	Points	PIMS	+/-
65	14	30	44	52	+16

Brent Benson was an extremely hyped forward going into the 2008 WHL Bantam Draft, and eventually went 6th Overall to the Saskatoon Blades. Despite being 6th Overall Brent was the second player Saskatoon selected; joining Duncan Siemens who was taken 3rd overall. Brent is in good company among the top 6, which also includes HockeyProspect.com's #1 pick, Ryan Nugent-Hopkins, along with Ty Rattie, Michael St. Croix, Mark McNeill, and of course the aforementioned Siemens.

Benson got a taste of the WHL in 4 games as a 15 year old. Then as a rookie he was caught behind several forwards on the Blades depth chart limiting his ice time. Nevertheless, he still managed to put up 8 goals and 18 points. Brent was expected to break out this season, and although he put up respectable point totals, he left something to be desired. Brent was very streaky throughout the season and kept leaving us wanting more, as he appeared to have it. Benson has respectable skating abilities, and is at his best when handling the puck and setting up offense. Along with his playmaking skills, Benson also has a deceptive shot, which he doesn't use consistently enough in appropriate places. We have seen Benson contribute in his own end, and has held his own in corner battles.

Benson has always been projected as a player with great potential. Up to this point he hasn't realized it. The talent is there, and whoever selects him will be going for that home run pick, because if he can put it all together on a consistent basis, Benson could become a very effective offensive contributor.

Shane McColgan

Right Wing – Kelowna Rockets (WHL)
Born Jan 1 1993 - Manhattan Beach, CA
Height 5.08 - Weight 165 - Shoots R

DRAFT GUIDE' 11

Games	Goals	Assists	Points	PIMS	+/-
67	21	45	66	62	+3

Shane McColgan was pegged by many as a 1st rounder going back to the pre-season. It's going to be tough for that to happen now. McColgan has had a pretty rough season and actually posted fewer points than last season, albeit with 4 games fewer played. The undersized forward posted 25 goals and 44 helpers as a rookie last season.

The Manhattan Beach, California native's stock will be an interesting one to watch when draft day arrives. HP's Mark Edwards spoke about Shane. "I went to Rochester in the summer and was looking forward to watching Shane live after seeing the numbers he posted last season. He didn't make a great first impression on me. He didn't play very smart. He was undersized of course, and had too many needless turnovers. I also saw him twice in Toronto and still didn't see first round talent. When a player is 5'9 which might even be generous in this case and around 160 pounds, I think he needs to be very dynamic player. I have not seen that in my viewings of him."

Hockey Prospects WHL scout, Jason Hills filed much the same scouting report. Shane is a speedy kid with scoring ability and has a bit of piss and vinegar in his game. McColgan might end up being a 3rd rounder with some good upside. He is the kind of player that can make scouts look really dumb down the road. His frame is not big, so it will be tough for him to add a ton of bulk. If he can play smarter and also get stronger and is able to win more battles along walls, it will go a long way to determining his career path. He had a solid 2011 playoffs.

Logan Shaw

RW– Cape Breton (QMJHL)
Born Oct 5 1992 - Glace Bay, NS
Height 6.03 - Weight 190 - Shoots R

Games	Goals	Assists	Points	PIMS	+/-
68	26	20	46	37	-18

Logan Shaw suited up with one of the worst offensive teams in the entire CHL. This didn't help Logan Shaw's statistics, but he still managed to get more than 20 goals during the season.

Shaw played with another big body in Cory MacIntosh. Both players really made a nice duo and their physical play on the ice really was their bread and butter against the opposing team's first defense unit.

Shaw is the natural scoring big power forward type. He goes to the front of the net and redirects rebounds or direct passes in the net. He's good at playing along the boards, and he has some good skills bringing the puck to the slot. He has a good quick release on his wrist shot that he uses pretty well.

Shaw has a pretty good stride and protects the puck well against the walls where he wins plenty of one on one battles. He has above average hands for a big kid. He has proven he can score and does a good job taking the puck wide on defensemen and then powering to the net while shielding the puck with his body.

We would like to see him make his decisions quicker in the offensive zone. Sometimes Shaw can try to do too much and cause turnovers high in the opposing territory. He is a dedicated player, but he still needs to work on his focus in the defensive zone on decisions making. He plays a rather simple game and he gets good speed in the neutral zone for a big kid. Shaw shows flashes of blue chip prospect some games and in other games you have trouble finding him. Is he a boom or bust pick?

Kale Kessy

Left Wing – Medicine Hat Tigers (WHL)
Born Dec 4 1992 - Shaunavon, SASK
Height 6.02 - Weight -184 - Shoots L

HOCKEYPROSPECT.COM
DRAFT GUIDE' 11

Games	Goals	Assists	Points	PIMS	+/-
65	10	14	24	129	+5

Ever since Milan Lucic emerged with his outstanding combination of size and skill, it seems every year someone in the WHL draws a comparison to him. This year, that someone is going to be Kale Kessy. We're not saying Kale will replicate Lucic's performance, but it's hard to ignore Kessy's great size and strength, especially considering how much he has grown.

Kale was passed over in the 2008 WHL Bantam Draft, and selected by the Medicine Hat Tigers as a "listed player". Kale made the choice to play "AAA" hockey with the Medicine Hat Tigers' Midget program. After putting up respectable totals, Kessy was brought in to play a few games at the WHL level at the end of that season. Kale put up very good numbers, especially for a player entering his first full season. Kale put up similar numbers this year, and had a good output of points during the playoffs; however his performance isn't strictly point based.

Kale combines some good offensive instincts in the goal area, and a good shot, with strong play in his own zone. Kessy is solid along the boards, so as a result he wins a ton of battles. Although Kessy racks up the penalty minutes, and drops the gloves on a regular basis, a lot of the fights we've seen have involved him standing up for a teammate, rather than running around looking to fight. Kessy appears to play the game with good integrity, and is an extremely hard worker.

We expect Kessy to take a full on power forward role with some graduations in Medicine Hat this season. We are very interested to see how he progresses as he could become a force in the WHL physically, both in front of the net, and in dropping the gloves.

Luke Hietkamp

Right Wing - Peterborough Petes (OHL)
Born Aug 15 1993 - London, ONT
Height 6.02 - Weight 196 - Shoots R

DRAFT GUIDE' 11

Games	Goals	Assists	Points	PIMS	+/-
55	6	4	10	42	-24

Luke Hietkamp was selected 26th overall on the 2009 OHL Priority Selection by the Peterborough Petes. Hietkamp played and starred with Boone Jenner with the Elgin-Middlesex Chiefs in his draft year. Jenner now plays for the Petes bitter rivals, the Oshawa Generals. Hietkamp made the Petes out of camp, and put together a respectable performance.

Hietkamp's development over the last two years has been affected by injuries. Since his return to the Petes line-up around mid-season, he has taken on a top six role. He has very quietly been a very valuable member of the Petes beyond the score sheet, specifically on the penalty kill, where he has showed maturity and ability in this role beyond his years and experience. In addition to plenty of penalty kill experience for the 17 year old forward, Hietkamp uses his close to NHL ready frame to punish opposing players along the boards, using this size to deliver hits, as well was win battles along the boards.

Hietkamp plays with a ton of determination and displays a strong forecheck. He does a lot of the little things right and makes extra effort plays that make a difference. Hietkamp has been seen, on multiple occasions, in pain on the ice after blocking a shot. He seems un-phased and continues to fearlessly throw himself in front of shots. The only knock on Hietkamp is that he lacks legitimate top six skill at the NHL level. However, with his great frame, determination, and ability to do a lot of the little things right, Hietkamp puts together a great combination of skills that could make him an excellent bottom six forward at the highest level.

Eddie Wittchow

Defense – Burnsville (H.S Minnesota)
Born Aug 13 1993 - Calgary, ALTA
Height 6.03 - Weight 185 - Shoots L

HOCKEYPROSPECT.COM

DRAFT GUIDE' 11

Games	Goals	Assists	Points	PIMS	+/-
25	9	14	23	28	NA

Each year, a few players seemingly come out of nowhere to surprise scouts. Such is the case with Minnesota high school defenseman Eddie Wittchow. HP was alerted to Wittchow last summer by an NCAA coach. Not only is Wittchow climbing the NHL draft boards, he is also a very accomplished lacrosse player. Wittchow is the star of both teams at Burnsville High School. One of his best assets is his footwork, a skill most certainly honed on the lacrosse field. While Mario Lucia may be the No. 1 rated Minnesota high school player, Wittchow may be the best player from the Land of 10,000, lakes flying under the radar.

For a player with excellent size, Wittchow has terrific skating ability. Not only does he have a quick first few steps, his top speed is very good as well. He has solid agility, and his lateral movement is well above average. Wittchow is also not afraid to use his sizable frame to knock opponents off the puck. He wins battles down low and in the corners and knows when to lay the body. His deficiencies come with some of the mental aspects of the game. He is a great athlete, but he needs to learn the game as his skills are very raw. He employs a pretty smart style now, but playing against better talent at higher levels will help to shore up his abilities.

Wittchow will likely be a longer-term project for an NHL franchise. He needs to work on things like gap control and positioning. With his speed and skill, he should have no problem picking up these things in the coming years. Wittchow will need seasoning at lower levels to gain more confidence and further his development before playing in the NHL. But he has a solid foundation that will make him appealing to teams. He has the ideal size, skill and toughness of a top-level defenseman.

David Broll

Left Wing – Soo Greyhounds (OHL)
Born January 4, 1993 -Mississauga, Ont.
Height 6.02 - Weight 216 - Shoots L

HOCKEYPROSPECT.COM

DRAFT GUIDE' 11

Games	Goals	Assists	Points	PIMS	+/-
65	13	21	34	85	-10

David Broll was selected 10th overall in the OHL Priority Selection by the Erie Otters. David Broll was the 1st of 8 players selected out of the Toronto Young Nationals program, and was one of the biggest players available at the time of the draft. Broll weighed in at a massive 6'1" - 220lb. for a minor midget player.

Broll put up respectable numbers in his rookie season. During his sophomore year, at the trade deadline, Broll was a key part of a deal that sent Brett Thompson to the Erie Otters, making Broll a Sault Ste. Marie Greyhound. The Soo already had heavily scouted prospects for the 2011 NHL Entry Draft including Daniel Catenacci, Nick Cousins, and Ryan Sproul. This probably meant for some extra exposure for Broll.

The first thing you notice when you see David Broll is his massive size. Broll uses this size both to physically punish and intimidate his opponents, and to battle in corners. Broll is a very difficult player to get past if he's engaging in a battle along the boards, as he wins a good percentage of battles. Broll has a decent shot, but not one with the force you'd expect out of someone Broll's size.

Going forward, Broll will need to vigorously work on his skating abilities if he wants a shot at an NHL career. Broll's size, physicality, and willingness to punish opposing players will likely be worth a mid-round pick on it's own. Whoever selects Broll will need to thoroughly help him improve his skating in order for him to become an effective NHL prospect.

Colin Miller

Defense – Soo Greyhounds (OHL)
Born Oct 29 1992 - Sault Ste. Marie, ON'
Height 6.01 - Weight 153 - Shoots R

HOCKEYPROSPECT.COM

DRAFT GUIDE' 11

Games	Goals	Assists	Points	PIMS	+/-
66	3	19	22	44	+2

Colin Miller came seemingly out of nowhere being signed as a free agent in May of 2010 by the Sault Ste. Marie Greyhounds. A native of Sault Ste. Marie, Miller stepped up his game and earned a roster spot out of camp. Miller showed at lower levels that he does have some offensive attributes, but in the OHL this year with the Greyhounds. Miller's primary role was defensive zone play, in which Miller did very well.

His positioning overall is very solid, and displays an active stick. Miller's skating is acceptable, but will require more work. Miller does a decent job along the boards despite not having a lot of strength. Miller's hard work pays off in this area. The concern of strength stems into other area's of Miller's game as he has shown on multiple occasions to have trouble handling players in front of his own net.

Miller could turn into a solid bottom pairing defenseman at the NHL level; however, he will need to add muscle to his 6'1" frame, while at the same time improving his skating which is marginally acceptable at this point of his development.

The path to the NHL will likely be long for Miller, but he has shown this year he has legitimate potential as a prospect, and is deserving of some draft consideration. We like the upside in this prospect.

Michael Mersch

Left Wing – Wisconsin (NCAA)
Born Oct 2 1992 - Park Ridge, IL
Height 6.01 - Weight 196 - Shoots L

Games	Goals	Assists	Points	PIMS	+/-
39	8	10	18	30	NA

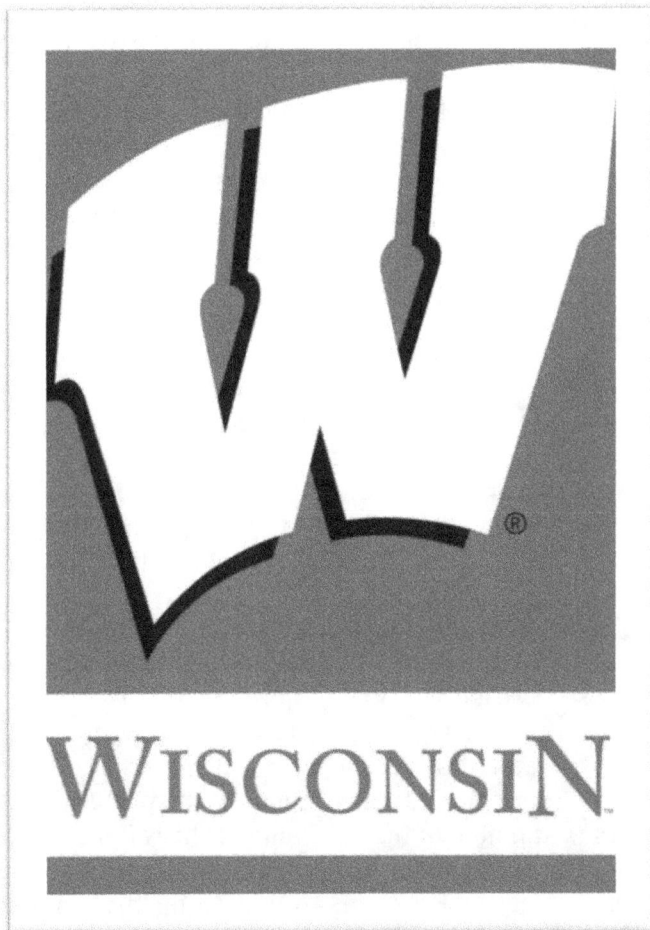

Michael Mersch came to to the Wisconsin Badgers after spending three years with the U.S. National Team Development Program. While with the USNTDP, he led the under-17 team with 27 goals in the 2008-09 season. Mike popped in 8 goals in his freshman year this season in the NCAA.

Mersch is a player we might have ranked higher than some. Mersch probably gets pushed down the rankings because of his lack of skating skill. He still gets around the rink well enough though and he makes up for his lack of skating skill in other ways. We really like Mike because he is a really smart hockey player. Much like the way we ignored Ryan O'Reilly's lack of high end skating prowess, Mersch fits that mold with HP.

Mersch has a good size frame so he does not lack the size to compete in the NHL. You can't teach hockey sense, or at minimum it is very difficult to teach it. This kid has a high hockey IQ, and it shoots him up our rankings.

Mike is a player that you can trust in all three zones. He competes every shift and has very soft hands, which is always a pleasure to see, especially when the player is 6'1, 200 lbs.

Garrett Meurs

RW/Center – Plymouth Whalers (OHL)
Born Jan 12 1993 - Ripley, ONT
Height 5.11 - Weight 170 - Shoots R

Games	Goals	Assists	Points	PIMS	+/-
68	10	30	40	61	+7

Meurs was selected 14th Overall in the 2009 OHL Priority Selection by the Plymouth Whalers out of the Huron-Perth Lakers program. Meurs headlined a solid draft crop out of Plymouth who also features fellow prospects Matt Mahalak, Stefan Noesen, Nick Malysa, and unreported forward J.T. Miller. Meurs made the team out of camp, and had a very successful rookie season, finishing 8th in points among all OHL rookies. Meurs looked poised to have a breakout season this year, and was projected fairly high at the start of the season. However this did not turn out to be the case, as Meurs actually regressed in the number of goals he would score this season, despite playing 6 more games, and receiving more ice time than the previous year.

Meurs seemed to be a player who made his presence known more as the game progressed. He consistently took some extra effort to find on the ice, as he was not very noticeable in most viewings early on in games. Meurs is player whose talent we respected all the way back to his days with Huron-Perth. Meurs is still able to display some of that offensive potential, particularly coming off the half-boards. Meurs is effective in handling opposing players along the walls, and is dangerous after winning a battle. He seems to find an open teammate quickly to setup scoring chance. Unfortunately Meurs has shown to be undisciplined at times trying to mix things up, but tends to deliver that extra shot that sees him land in the penalty box.

Garrett Meurs has good hands, some offensive instincts, and can be a physical player when a hit is available. However, we have a tough time getting over his inconsistent play this season. There are clearly some assets to Garrett that make him a potentially solid prospect. However, his stock has fallen drastically this season. The positive thing for Meurs is that he has too much talent to be passed up. If he can play with more drive and determination, Garrett could be a valuable mid round pick-up.

Mitchell Heard

Center– Plymouth Whalers (OHL)
Born Mar 12 1992 - Bowmanville, ONT
Height 6.02 - Weight -180 - Shoots L

Games	Goals	Assists	Points	PIMS	+/-
66	19	29	48	67	+4

The value of a good faceoff man is sometimes overlooked. Mitchell Heard is a very good faceoff man. Heard came to the Whalers via the now defunct Bowmanville Eagles of the OJHL. The 1992 born player was basically a rookie this season for Plymouth as he only played 16 games for them in the 2009/2010 season. Heard entered this season as a 'second time around' prospect as far as the NHL Draft is concerned. He was eligible last year as a May 92' birthdate.

Heard brings value as a very solid overall player. He is never going to be a top 6 forward in the NHL but he does have some scoring talent and, as we mentioned earlier, his faceoff skills are outstanding. There are players who can make a living playing in the NHL by winning faceoffs and being responsible in all three zones. Mitchell is that type of player.

Heard is a decent skater. He won't wow anyone with his skating skills but they are not a stopper as far as the NHL goes. He is a hard worker and plays a pretty smart game all over he ice. As we mentioned, he has scoring ability. He had a game in Brampton this year which showed off above average hands and scoring abilities. He could surprise down the road in the points department.

Mitchell Heard is a work in progress. He has just under 100 games of OHL experience as he awaits this years draft in June. We loved his production and the progress he showed as a prospect this season and expect him to be a valuable player for the Whalers going forward. HP's Mark Edwards gives the last word on Heard: "I liked him more with each viewing. He had some grit and can chip in on the score sheet. I think he is probably worthy of a draft pick based on his work in the faceoff circle alone. I would draft this kid."

Andrey Pedan

Defense – Guelph Storm (OHL)
Born Jul 3 1993 - Moscow, Russia
Height 6.04 - Weight 201 - Shoots L

Games	Goals	Assists	Points	PIMS	+/-
51	2	10	12	89	-11

Andrey Pedan was selected high in both the CHL Import draft, and by his hometown team in the first round of the KHL Entry Draft. After some deliberation, Pedan chose to join the Guelph Storm who selected him 1st Round, 32nd Overall. Pedan made quick adjustments to the OHL, thanks to his huge size, and take no prisoners attitude around throwing his 6'4" 200 pound body around. Pedan plays a North American style of game.

Pedan is highlighted by his physical play. However, he needs to apply this within the rules of the game, as he constantly finds himself tagged with penalties with such as "roughing" "checking to the head" and "boarding", which at times has happened during important points of the game. This can be a double hit to his team as not only does it put them short-handed, but Pedan has been relied upon in a defensive role on a semi-regular basis.

Pedan can best be described as a "raw" prospect as he shows elements such as size, physicality and defensive awareness in his defensive game, but needs to be more polished and improve several small areas in his game. Pedan's skating is respectable but could end up being the make or break point moving forward. Without question, Pedan needs to get stronger on his skates to play at the top level. Offensively Pedan doesn't show a great deal of upside, however he does have a huge point shot.

HP Scout Ryan Yessie elaborates on Pedan: "Pedan plays a very North American style of game. I love his physicality, and willingness to mix it up, but not his bad penalties at key points of the game. Next year will be huge for Pedan as his role in Guelph expands with the loss of Van Laren and Lofquist, if not more on their back end."

Carter Sandlak

Left Wing – Belleville Bulls (OHL)
Born May 18 1993 - London, ONT
Height 6.02 – Weight- 190 - Shoots L

Games	Goals	Assists	Points	PIMS	+/-
56	13	10	23	69	-15

Some players are attractive to teams and scouts not because they have amazing skills, but because they do all of the little things well. The son of ex-NHL'er and current Ducks scout, Jim, Carter Sandlak is a jack-of-all-trades type of player. He does not blow you away with skill, but he does not have any glaring weaknesses either. There are a few things that he does have, including size and a solid work ethic.

Sandlak has not put up great numbers, but it is certainly not for a lack of effort. He is a fierce competitor who battles along the boards and plays a smart game. His positioning is terrific, and he has a solid hockey IQ. Sandlak is not a fantastic skater but does a solid job for his size. At 6-foot-2 and 190 pounds, Sandlak can be a physical force. He is not afraid to lay the body or drop the gloves. Defensively, he has solid instincts and knows where to be most of the time. When he finds himself out of position, his dogged work ethic helps him to correct the error. With some schooling on the offensive side and an increase in confidence, Sandlak could be a power forward in the making. He keeps his stick on the ice and battles in the dirty areas. He will not surprise anyone with a blistering wrist shot, but he is capable of scoring the garbage goals in front of the net.

Because of the role he plays for Belleville, it is probably fair to project Sandlak as a third or fourth line energy player at the NHL level. He will chip in some offense here and there, but his game will revolve around delivering hits, forechecking, playing defense, wearing on the opposition and playing an intelligent style. If a team is patient and allows Sandlak to develop further, he may be a solid NHL player.

Austen Brassard

Right Wing– Belleville Bulls (OHL)
Born Jan 14 1993 - Windsor, ONT
Height 6.02 - Weight 191 - Shoots R

DRAFT GUIDE' 11

Games	Goals	Assists	Points	PIMS	+/-
67	19	15	34	78	-19

Expectations of Belleville Bulls winger Austen Brassard have been very high since the beginning of the year. Some scouts had Brassard as a first-round selection. He brings a lot of solid attributes to the table, including great size, hockey sense, positional play and a competitive attitude. At 6-foot-2 and 190 pounds, Brassard has ideal size and has been getting stronger over the past few seasons. With an even greater dedication to developing physically, Brassard could be a talented power forward.

He has good offensive skills, but his numbers do not reflect the type of praise he was receiving early in the season. Brassard has a good shot but does not have the killer instinct to bury a ton of goals. Because he does not have the offensive prowess of some of the other top prospects, his stock could fall a bit. His passing skills are average as well. However, Brassard's hockey IQ is very high. He is extremely sound positional wise and has good defensive instincts. He battles for loose pucks and is strong in his board play. His skating skills are average, and he does not have great speed or quickness. Mediocre mobility coupled with decent skills means that Brassard will need to be extra diligent in his approach to getting better.

While Brassard might have been a bit over-hyped at the beginning of the season resulting in many being disappointed in his play, he still has a lot of potential. His skills are solid and with his work ethic, he will only get better as time goes along. Brassard projects as a very good energy player and with patience from an NHL franchise, he could develop into a nice NHL player. He just might not be the first-round talent many expected.

Mike Morrison

Goalie – Kitchener Rangers (OHL)
Born Nov 7 1992 - Hamilton, ONT
Height 6.00 – Weight - 177 - Catches L

Games	Wins	Losses	G.A.A	Save %	SO
27	15	6	2.65	.912	2

Many people in hockey circles believe that goaltenders take the longest to develop. There may be any number of reasons for this. In most cases, as a goalie gains more experience, the promising prospects settle in quite nicely and often reach their potential. Michael Morrison, a goaltender for the Kitchener Rangers of the Ontario Hockey League, has seen his goals against average decrease in each of his OHL seasons. His save percentage has increased as well, something that will catch the eye of NHL franchises.

Morrison has average size at 6-foot and 175 pounds, but he is a terrific athlete. His lateral quickness and overall positioning are tremendous. Like many young goaltenders, Morrison's deficiencies come from rebound control and vision. He gives up way too many rebounds and has been saved by his solid Kitchener defensive corps on more than one occasion. He seems to be bothered by any traffic in front of the net while struggling to maintain sight of the puck. With players crashing the net on a regular basis in the NHL, Morrison will need to rectify this situation in a hurry. He looks uncomfortable at times seeing the puck even without traffic, something that does not bode well for his draft stock.

While some of his technical skills are questionable, Morrison remains a solid prospect because of his athleticism. He can overcome some of his mechanical mistakes by making an acrobatic save, but he will not be able to rely on physical skills alone in the NHL. Morrison will be a project that needs seasoning at the lower levels. He has all of the physical tools, and if he can improve the technical aspects of playing goalie at the highest level, he could be a good player in the NHL. Mike may get increased playing time next season. We already think that he was the best goalie in Kitchener this season.

Seth Griffith

Center /RW– London Knights (OHL)
Born Jan 4 1993 - Wallaceburg, ONT
Height 5.10 - Weight 185 - Shoots R

HOCKEYPROSPECT.COM

DRAFT GUIDE' 11

Games	Goals	Assists	Points	PIMS	+/-
68	22	40	62	28	-1

Despite being just 5-foot-10 and 185 pounds, London Knights center Seth Griffith is able to put the puck in the net. Griffith plays in front of the net on the power play and goes to the dirty areas to score. Many players make the mistake of doing a fly-by or not staying in front of the net for rebounds, but Griffith charges hard to the net on the rush. He provides a lot of energy and has some solid offensive skills. His ability to make plays on the power play has resulted in a lot of goals for his team. He has terrific passing ability.

Griffith is a good forechecker. That allows him to create problems for defenders. His tenacious attitude and work ethic make life miserable for opponents. If he was bigger, he would undoubtedly be even more effective with the style of game he plays. Griffith struggles with consistency. One night he looks like a game-breaking player, and the next he might not do much at all. He is a solid skater with good speed and quickness. Griffith's shot is also pretty good, but he scores many of his goals from close range.

Seth will need to be a bit tougher chasing down pucks along the walls. We saw him 'pull the shute' a few times. This is not uncommon amongst some younger, smaller players though. While Seth has put up solid numbers this year, he projects as more of an energy player at the NHL level. If he continues to improve his play on the defensive side of the puck, he could be a solid depth player in the NHL and might surprise some with his skill.

Dylan DeMelo

Defense – Mississauga Majors (OHL)
Born May 1 1993 - London, ONT
Height 6.01 – Weight - 199 - Shoots R

Games	Goals	Assists	Points	PIMS	+/-
67	3	24	27	70	+31

As with any draft, there are a few players in this year's class that do not quite have the same exposure as others. Mississauga defenseman Dylan DeMelo is one such player. Playing on one of the best teams in the Ontario Hockey League limits his ice time and has perhaps stunted his growth a bit. While watching others and studying their games is certainly beneficial, learning from experience and playing are the best teachers.

DeMelo is not huge but has good size at 6'1" and 193 pounds. He works hard along the boards and wins a lot of battles because of his compete level. He will need to get much stronger to play against top-level competition, but that will come with time. Because DeMelo still needs to learn the game a bit. As a result of not playing a ton of minutes, he could be a longer-term project for a team drafting him. DeMelo needs to improve his defensive positioning. With that said, he shows a lot of the tools that make a successful NHL defenseman. He battles hard and can take and deliver punishment. Despite only scoring 3 goals, DeMelo has some nice offensive upside as well. He possesses a hard, accurate shot and is capable as a passer.

DeMelo has the work ethic and commitment to playing the body. It could earn him an NHL roster spot in the future. He needs to gain more confidence and learn positioning better if he hopes to play at the highest level. DeMelo will not step into the NHL for a few years, but he could be a promising prospect as he garners more experience with one of the best teams in Canadian junior hockey.

Shane Prince

Left Wing- Ottawa 67's (OHL)
Born Nov 16 1992 - Spencerport, NY
Height 5.10 - Weight 174 - Shoots L

HOCKEYPROSPECT.COM

DRAFT GUIDE'11

Games	Goals	Assists	Points	PIMS	+/-
59	25	63	88	18	+43

One of the most important things that NHL franchises have to take into account is that players who are prolific junior hockey scorers do not always translate to scorers in the NHL. Such could be the case with Shane Prince of the Ottawa 67's in the Ontario Hockey League. The sub-six footer finishes every check with authority. He is a good skater and can rush the puck into the offensive zone. Prince is a dynamic forechecker and creates scoring opportunities with his pressure on defenders.

Prince wins a lot of battles along the boards due to his abrasive style, but he gets himself into trouble because he takes shifts off. At times, Prince looks very disinterested in playing defense. He has all of the tools to be a solid two-way player, but the engagement level is not always where it needs to be. Offensively, he has a lot of solid skills. He has a good shot and racks up assist numbers with his passing ability. Prince is prone to trying to do too much and can turn over pucks because of it. He plays a nice physical game but he tries to get fancy too often. He struggles to create on his own, but playing with players like Ryan Martindale and Tyler Toffoli wouldn't hurt any player. This could have inflated his statistics a bit. It is always important to remember who players play with and the ice time they are given. It deserves some consideration when projecting offensive potential. Columbus drafted Dalton Smith 34th overall last season. His point production dropped off this year with Shane Prince taking shifts on the Toffoli and Martindale line. Prince does deserve credit for producing when he was given the chance to succeed.

While his point production might suggest that he will be a top-six forward at the NHL level, Prince seems to project more as a solid third-line player. He may give a team a forechecking presence up front and chip in with some offence. He needs heavy defensive schooling and must make the effort to get better and more consistent in all three zones.

Philippe Maillet

Center– Victoriaville Tigres (QMJHL)
Born Nov 7 1992 - Lachenaie, PQ
Height 5.09 - Weight 174 - Shoots L

Games	Goals	Assists	Points	PIMS	+/-
67	31	38	69	17	+7

Philippe Maillet is yet another highly scouted offensive center in Victoriaville. Every scout will look at his size first and be a bit disappointed, but the 5'9" 174 pound prospect is just fine at working against the big guys with his small frame. He uses great quickness and very good speed to create a lot of chances for himself and his teammates.

Maillet's execution with the puck is almost perfect. He has a lot of skill and precision in what he does, and he rarely skates himself into a corner with the puck. Philippe has good patience and also has his head up to see what's going on in all 3 zones. He positions himself in a way that creates lanes for his teammates and uses his elusiveness to get away from defensive coverage. Speed, hard work and intelligence has been a huge factor in most of his points.

Like every small, speedy, skilled forward, he needs to get stronger in his battles on the boards. When you can direct him to the walls, you can limit the damage that he will do offensively. He doesn't shy away from physical play but he is certainly not the best small player to handle it. We would like to see him get more involved in battles in front of the net to get a few dirty goals, and see a bit less of him trying to just dangle around defensemen. Sometimes players need to simplify their game in order to be effective and we believe that in some cases it would be a benefit for him and for his team to do just that. He's alright with big guys in the Q as he is faster than the majority of them, but he definitely needs more pounds on his frame to win the battles on the boards at a higher level.

Guillaume Cloutier

Defense– Chicoutimi (QMJHL)
Born Feb 18 1993 - St-Constant, PQ
Height 6.02 - Weight 170 - Shoots R

Games	Goals	Assists	Points	PIMS	+/-
62	3	9	12	30	+15

The 17 year old defenseman was traded from the powerful St-John Sea Dogs to the Chicoutimi Saguenéens during the Christmas break and it has helped him get more quality ice time. Cloutier responded to every challenge that coach Guy Carbonneau has gave him. Cloutier is not a flashy defenseman by any means, but he can do anything and adapt to every situation, that's his main strength.

Cloutier has a nice frame at 6' 2" 170 pounds. He can skate with the best of them. He is pretty aggressive in his gap control. He just needs to be careful with the position of his stick when he gets too aggressive trying cut the inside lane on players. Cloutier is physical, he hits pretty hard, and he likes to do it when players take the puck to the wide side of the ice. He has good timing. His passes and decisions are intelligent on the ice, not causing turnovers and rarely getting caught out of position. He likes to uses his speed on the powerplay to get himself to the backdoor. He creates a lot of opportunities with his mobility.

Cloutier needs to work on a few parts of his game. One thing is his poise with the puck. The more he gets comfortable with handling the puck, the more time he will give the forwards to setup for a play down-low in the offensive zone. Too often he just puts the puck back on the half-boards even though it's not available. He also needs to practice both his slap shot and wrist shot. He needs to work on speeding up his release to get pucks to the net faster. Cloutier is a pretty solid prospect with good upside. If he improves in a few areas we mentioned above it will go along way towards determining how far he goes in his career.

Marcel Noebels

LW – Seattle Thunderbirds (WHL)
Born Mar 14 1992, Germany
Height 6.02 - Weight 195 - Shoots L

Games	Goals	Assists	Points	PIMS	+/-
66	28	26	54	23	-11

Marcel split last year between the DEL (German top league) and the DNL (German U-18 league) for the Krefeld Penguine. After the season was over Noebels went on to absolutely dominate the WJC U-18 Championships with Norway/Toronto Maple Leafs' prospect Sondre Olden, and fellow 2011 Eligible Nicklas Jensen (Oshawa). Noebels put up 9G, 10A in only 5 games.

Despite all of this, Noebels was passed over in the 2010 NHL Entry Draft and felt that making the jump to the CHL would improve his draft stock, and did it ever. Noebels was selected 10th overall in the CHL Import Draft, and made an immediate impact with the Seattle Thunderbirds putting in just over a point per game as a rookie. Then, put on a solid performance for Germany at the World Junior Championships winning the "Top 3 player on team" award for Germany. Noebels returned to where he left off, seeing him shoot up the rankings becoming the undisputed top re-entry player for the 2011 NHL Entry Draft.

Despite being a European rookie in the WHL, Noebels wears an "A" for Seattle. Noebels is a very creative player with the puck, and has good hands allowing him to create offense. He displays a solid shot, and good ability to get open to utilize it. Noebels likes to carry the puck, and prefers to stickhandle right to the net where he has shown some good moves. However, despite all of this, Noebels has shown the lack of willingness to play into the dirty areas of the ice. He will dish the puck off at times if he thinks he could get hit. He tends to stay away from the corners, and the boards. This has become a bigger concern when watching him in more physical games. Considering his size, he has the ability to adapt, and it may just be an adjustment to a different style of game. If Noebels can make the adjustment to a more physical brand of hockey, he could have a bright future ahead of him on North American ice.

Liam Liston

Goalie– Brandon (WHL)
Born Apr 6 1993 - London, ON, CAN
Height 6.00 - Weight 191 - Catches L

Games	Wins	Losses	G.A.A	Save %	SO
41	20	16	3.77	.880	1

Liston is a goaltender who recently completed his first season for the Brandon Wheat Kings of the WHL. It was looking like a tough task to ask any goaltender to step into. The Wheat Kings were clearly in more of a rebuild mode after hosting the Memorial Cup last season. The Wheat Kings surprised many by finishing with a record around the .500 mark. Liston played the greater share of games for Brandon during the regular season and posted a very respectable 20 wins but only played one game in the playoffs. It's not exactly how you envision the end of your draft year season to go when you draw it up. His season could be described as "all over the place". He had stellar moments and other points in his rookie season were more forgettable. An .880 save percentage is not exactly a target number for any goalie, let alone a young tender looking to get drafted into the NHL.

At 6'2" and 202 pounds, Liston has the size that NHL teams seek these days. He is pretty solid technically and moves around his net really well, especially given his huge frame. He showed hiccups with both hands (blocker and glove), but they are not awful. He challenges shooters more often than not. It's our opinion that Liam's season is just the result of a young goalie learning and developing at a position known for late bloomers. The hiccups are most likely do to lack of maturity and experience. Mark Visentin struggled in his rookie season too.

Liston has the frame of an NHL goalie, but needs to work on his consistency. He earned himself an invite to the CHL Top Prospects game this season, where he didn't give up a goal. Liston was a third round pick in the 2008 WHL Bantam Draft and will look to work on his consistency heading into next season. Liston mentioned Cam Ward as an NHL goalie he looks to pattern his game after stating that he shares the same general style. Liston is worth drafting on his measurables alone.

Luke Lockhart

RW/Center– Seattle Thunderbirds (WH
Born Nov 1 1992 - Burnaby, BC
Height 5.10 - Weight 180 - Shoots R

Games	Goals	Assists	Points	PIMS	+/-
71	21	27	48	27	-14

Luke Lockhart was taken in the 7th round of the 2007 WHL Bantam Draft by the Seattle Thunderbirds. Lockhart proved his value quickly as he combined good energy and speed, with a little bit of a scoring touch to put together two respectable seasons for a small, young player who was selected midway through the draft. Luke has really come into his own offensively, producing at a fairly consistent rate, and playing with a lot of energy.

Luke displays good skating ability, has good hands, and can be fairly elusive and shifty when he's driving to the goal. Lockhart hasn't been afraid to drive right to the net, and we've seen him capitalize in key moments due to his fearless nature. Lockhart seems to play every shift with a lot of energy and push hard to try and help his team out. Luke has the ability to complete high difficulty passes on fairly regular basis. He is very composed with the puck under pressure.

Despite not winning all his battles in the corners, Lockhart has shown a willingness to go into the corners, go along the boards and battle for the puck, and has been willing to take punishment. We hope to see him add some muscle to his frame, to maximize his potential.

Jonathan Racine

Defense - Shawinigan (QMJHL)
Born May 28 1993 - Montreal, PQ
Height 6.01 - Weight 182 - Shoots L

HOCKEYPROSPECT.COM

DRAFT GUIDE' 11

Games	Goals	Assists	Points	PIMS	+/-
68	2	5	7	86	0

The impressive thing you notice pretty quickly when making a scouting trip to watch Racine, is that the 17 year old is always on the ice versus the opposing team's top line. That's something pretty impressive considering the veteran defensive core in Shawinigan.

Without the puck, Racine is one of the most solid defenseman in the QMJHL for this draft. Racine has a nice big frame at 6'1" 182 pounds. He'll surely add some pounds during his summer training. Racine is a really hard young man to play against. He does not do anything extraordinary, but works hard all game long and plays with a real mean streak.

Racine uses his body well to to pin opponents on the boards and his positioning is good at all times in the defensive zone. This gives him the opportunity to cut down a lot of scoring chances by blocking shots and putting his stick in lanes to block cross-ice passes.

Racine plays 1-on-1 situations pretty well. He always closes his gap and pushes the opponent to the outside, and almost never gets beat with fancy moves. He can sometimes lose a guy with speed going wide on him. He is more than willing to mix it up when needed to protect his teammates, and he seems to be a good leader at a young age. Racine needs more speed to keep up with the best skaters in the league.

Racine really needs to gain more confidence with the puck. He needs to work on his passes and play with the puck. It can only get better and if he improves his puck skills and his decisions with the puck he will have a very solid game. Upside is big shutdown defenseman who plays mean. If his hands and decisions with the puck get better, he could be a steal if picked later in the draft.

Cason Hohmann

Center – Cedar Rapids (USHL)
Born Jan 10 1993 - Plymouth, MI
Height 5.08 - Weight 160 - Shoots R

Games	Goals	Assists	Points	PIMS	+/-
55	22	33	55	22	+19

Cedar Rapids Roughriders center Cason Hohmann has had to battle for every opportunity in his hockey career. At a diminutive 5-foot-8 and 160 pounds, Hohmann has to play much bigger to succeed in the United States' top junior league. But do not be fooled by his small stature. While he may be little in size, he makes up for that with terrific effort. His work ethic and dedication are two aspects that cannot be questioned.

Most small players have to be able to skate and score to be effective. Hohmann is no exception. He has blazing speed. His first few steps are terrific, and he has elite top-end speed and quickness. As one might expect, Hohmann has good hands as well. Never afraid to fire the puck on net, Hohmann has a knack for scoring goals. But while his skills have allowed him to excel at the United States Hockey League level, it is apparent that he will need to get even better to succeed in college and the NHL. The Texas native has committed to play for Boston University.

Size is undoubtedly Hohmann's biggest obstacle. To become a professional, he must hone his skills even further. He struggles along the walls and in the corners, and that will only be exposed more at higher levels. Hohmann will need to continue to display that tireless work ethic if he hopes to play in the NHL one day. He will likely be a long-term project that will not play in the NHL for a few years if at all. Many scouts think his size and good-but-not-great skills will prohibit him from being a factor in the NHL. Hohmann has had to prove people wrong for his entire life, and he will have to yet again to realize his dream.

Jean-Gabriel Pageau

Center – Gatineau Olympiques (QMJHL)
Born Nov 11 1992 - Ottawa, ONT
Height 5.09 - Weight 164 - Shoots R

HOCKEYPROSPECT.COM

DRAFT GUIDE' 11

Games	Goals	Assists	Points	PIMS	+/-
67	32	47	79	22	+23

The Gatineau Olympiques always seem to be able to develop players that no other teams were able to get. Pageau is not Claude Giroux, another gem from the Olympiques system, but he has a lot of similarities to him. They are both smaller, speedy, intelligent and skilled forwards.

Pageau has really stepped up his offensive game this season. He uses intelligence and an intense game mixed with good skills with the puck to make him an offensive force. Pageau has great breakaway speed. We have seen him show it off on many occasions. He is able to separate himself from defenders with a very quick burst. He battles very hard even though he's only 5'9" and he has pretty good strength for his size. He is one of those smaller forwards that plays much bigger than his listed weight. Having said that, we would still like to see him add a couple of pounds on that frame as it would really help his chances of reaching the NHL.

He finds the quiet areas on the ice to score goals and he is good at making himself invisible because he's always moving his feet in the offensive zone. This can make things very tough for defenseman to track him. He has a very good wrist shot and the explosiveness to break loose in the offensive zone. He is very good off the rush where he gets a chance to show off his creativity.

In his own zone, he is willing to sacrifice himself, but sometimes gets himself into trouble by running around a little too much. He loses his man in coverage at times. He will need to make sure to work hard on his play in his own zone going forward. Smaller forwards need to be a little more perfect in their overall game than bigger forwards when it comes to making it to the NHL.

We really like Pageau. It's a shame he is slighly undersized. Give him two inches and 20 pounds and he is a top 10 talent. We still think he could possibly end up being a draft day steal for some NHL team this June.

Yannick Veilleux

Left Wing– Shawinigan (QMJHL)
Born Feb 22 1993 - St-Hipolytte, PQ
Height 6.02 - Weight 190 - Shoots L

HOCKEYPROSPECT.COM

DRAFT GUIDE' 11

Games	Goals	Assists	Points	PIMS	+/-
68	19	29	48	40	-9

Yannick Veilleux is a talented young power forward that has put a lot of points up when playing on the same line as Montreal Canadiens' prospect Michael Bournival. Just like Bournival, he wins battles and competes as hard as he can on every shift. He has been able to stay on the first two lines all season long in a veteran-led team in Shawinigan as they try to make it to the Presidents Cup again this season.

He is a good strong player that is not the typical QMJHL speedy and skilled player. He is a power forward that uses his physical attributes to create plays. Veilleux is a big kid with very good puck protection skills. He has a good flow in his skating. It is very fluid and he can change direction pretty quickly and with his big body, defenseman have a tough time handling him. He has a good nose for the net and at only 17 years of age he doesn't lose a whole lot of battles against older players. I'd like to see him shoot a little bit more as he has nice vision, but can get away from what a true power forward should be about. He likes to throw hits, and isn't afraid to rough it up when necessary.

He needs to improve a bit in his own zone, be more mature in the breakouts; he tends to try dangerous plays at the blue line and use the middle of the ice a bit too much. Getting more maturity and experience will certainly help him in his decision making in his own zone. He also needs to add some quickness to his game. Up front, talent and strength speaks for this young man.

Ben Thomson

Left Wing – Kitchener Rangers (OHL)
Born Jan 16 1993 - Orangeville, ONT
Height 6.03 - Weight 205 - Shoots L

Games	Goals	Assists	Points	PIMS	+/-
68	6	13	19	107	-7

Thomson was selected in the 8th round of the 2009 OHL Priority Selection by Kitchener, and has panned out much better than the average mid round pick. Thomson started off well with limited ice time playing for the Rangers as a 16 year old. He put up 6 goals and 12 points and quietly showed his physical side. He took on a larger role with the team this season playing consistently on the 3rd line while being bumped up occasionally.

If you look at Thomson's measurements you can get a good idea of the type of player he is. He has great size and uses it pretty well most nights. He throws a lot of clean textbook checks that are extremely powerful. His size is used very efficiently in Kitchener, as he constantly battles along the boards, and wins. He is also extremely difficult to move from the front of the net on the power play, where he saw a respectable amount of time. In addition to this, Thomson has dropped the gloves more than a few times this year, and if anything, has shown how good he can be in this department, landing one of the biggest knockouts of anyone this year in the CHL to fellow draft prospect Barclay Goodrow. Ben sent the message to the many scouts in attendance that afternoon, that he can not only play physical, but can throw down as well.

Thomson appears to be a bit of a project with some untapped offensive potential. He has good hand-eye coordination, has shown good patience and composure with the puck at times, and has a massive slap shot which does not get used enough. Because Thomson understands his role he sticks to the physical side of the game, but if thrown in an elevated role where he is responsible for producing offense, he has shown signs of having skills capable to produce points. So as he moves up the depth chart in Kitchener, we may see some untapped abilities in Thomson. Moving forward we'd like to see Thomson improve his skating. It's not bad for a player his size, but could stand some improvement. Finally, the thing we would like to see from Ben is for him to play at a high level more often. We scout games in Kitchener often, and there were games that Ben hurt his draft stock with less than stellar efforts. All things considered, Ben is a legit NHL prospect.

Steven Trojanovic

Defense– Peterborough Petes (OHL)
Born Aug 4 1993 - Burlington, ONT
Height 6.01 - Weight 198 - Shoots R

HOCKEYPROSPECT.COM

DRAFT GUIDE' 11

Games	Goals	Assists	Points	PIMS	+/-
54	2	15	17	53	+5

Steven Trojanovic was selected by the Windsor Spitfires in the 3rd round of the 2009 OHL Priority Selection. Steven played sparingly for the Spitfires in 2009-2010 while spending most of his season with the Oakville Blades, and parts with the LaSalle Viper. Trojanovic started the year with Windsor, not gaining a great deal of ice time. He was eventually dealt to the Peterborough Petes three days before the OHL trade deadline in exchange for Adrian Robertson and a 2nd Round Pick. It was in Peterborough where he very quickly began receiving key minutes, and he was able to play top minutes, in all game situations.

Trojanovic combines his size, with relatively decent skating abilities. Despite not having ideal numbers for a player with his offensive skillset, he is a respectable prospect for this year's NHL Entry Draft.

Trojanovic has good top speed and his mobility is very good, especially on the point. He is at his best when quarterbacking the power play, as his puck movement is very efficient. He also makes sure he gets his shots on net. Trojanovic can take the puck up the ice effectively, and gain the offensive zone with his puck carrying ability. Despite having two-way potential on the blue line, Trojanovic plays a fairly offensive minded game. He will attempt to pinch and hold the line at times and has made too many bad reads in this regard.

In his own zone, Steven shows decent awareness and positioning, and throws the occasional hit. Considering his size, we would like to see more intensity and physicality out of him on a more regular basis. He can usually get the puck out of his own zone effectively, but will make the occasional bad play with the puck. He shows the determination to make up for his mistakes. Trojanovic is a project prospect moving forward who has the tools, but just needs to refine his game a bit more.

Josh Graves

Left Wing– Oshawa Generals (OHL)
Born Sep 26 1992 - Barrie, ONT
Height 6.03 - Weight 182 Shoots L

HOCKEYPROSPECT.COM

DRAFT GUIDE' 11

Games	Goals	Assists	Points	PIMS	+/-
52	5	10	15	37	-14

We first saw Graves play for Collingwood of the OJHL and were impressed with his play. Passed over in the 2009 OHL Priority Selection, Josh Graves was invited to the Oshawa Generals main camp in September 2010. He continuously put the puck in the net in exhibition action, and ended up making the team. Josh proceeded to put up 5 goals and 15 points through 52 games; not great numbers, but considering the lack of ice time, it is respectable production for a rookie caught behind several good scorers.

Josh has very good skating ability for a player his size. He has a very big frame in which he will still be able to add plenty of muscle to. Graves is a player who finishes his checks regularly, however. he isn't an overly physical player. He has shown good hands and has done fairly well in 1 on 1 situations, and is learning to use his size to protect the puck. Josh also has an underrated release on his shot.

What we really like about Josh is his great work ethic. With top players like Thomas, Jensen, Jenner, Lessio and Berger to name a few, and say that Graves was caught behind some talented players on the depth chart is a huge understatement. He didn't receive a ton of ice in the playoffs but when they needed to call on some of their depth players, Graves produced some points. Graves posted a third of his totals in only 9 playoff games. Graves seemed to prevail through limited minutes and make the most of what he got. There's a lot of potential going forward for Josh if an NHL team sees his potential.

HP scout Ryan Yessie on Graves: "I was able to catch a lot of Oshawa games this year. Every game I left impressed with Graves. He had a consistent work ethic, an underrated offensive skill set and is a true under the radar guy who exemplifies the reason HockeyProspect.com was created. If Graves played on a team without this kind of depth, his potential would have been more evident."

J.F Leblanc

Center – Val d'Or Foreurs (QMJHL)
Born Mar 3 1993 - St-Hyacinthe, PQ
Height 6.04 - Weight 190 - Shoots L

DRAFT GUIDE' 11

Games	Goals	Assists	Points	PIMS	+/-
63	19	32	51	40	-36

J.F Leblanc is a big tall kid listed at 6' 4". He has plenty of room to fill out as he is currently weighing in at 192 pounds. The former 1st rounder for the Foreurs has found his offensive game this season with his much improved abilities in the skating department.

He has a pretty good point production considering the Foreurs aren't an offensive force in the Q. He uses his long reach pretty well to create turnovers and he has really good talent with the puck. He doesn't play a big men's game, as he prefers the skilled game, but with his tall body it gives an interesting mix.

Leblanc can be pretty ineffective in physical games because he can't find his rhythm and he does not appear to be the biggest fan of body contact. He has lost battles along to walls against smaller more physical players far too often. No scouts want to see a player with his size play small. He really needs to improve this to be considered seriously as an NHL prospect.

He is an intelligent player though, he has solid enough skating ability and he cuts down lanes with his stick in the defensive zone. He has nice anticipation skills on the ice. He reads the play well.

Leblanc is patient with the puck and can create some good scoring chances with his great vision on the ice. The skilled 17 years old could become a very complete player with increased toughness and much more willingness to engage in the physical play. That along with adding more pounds to his frame would go a long way towards increasing his stock as an NHL prospect.

Reece Scarlett

Defense – Swift Current (WHL)
Born Mar 31 1993 - Edmonton, AB
Height 6.00 - Weight 165 - Shoots R

Games	Goals	Assists	Points	PIMS	+/-
72	6	18	24	59	-37

Reece Scarlett was drafted 12th overall by the Swift Current Broncos in the 2008 WHL Bantam Draft. Scarlett, a native of Sherwood Park, Alberta joined the Broncos for one game as a 15 year old, before playing full time as a rookie. He put up decent numbers for a rookie, and was expected to explode offensively this season. However, this did not happen, partially due to a lack of offense as a whole by Swift Current, who was 3rd worst in the WHL in goals scored.

Scarlett plays on a somewhat depleted Broncos' blue line, which sees him put in significant roles and situations that not all defensemen his age experience on a regular basis. Scarlett who is pushing 6'1" desperately needs to add muscle to his frame as he is a very slight 165 pounds. Scarlett posted respectable point totals this year, and will look to increase these again this year, as a key part of the organization's offensive development.

Reece is a smart defenseman, who chooses his positioning well, and has shown excellent decision making abilities. He doesn't hesitate to rush the puck up the ice whenever possible, and does so fairly effectively. At the same time, he recognizes and utilizes the right option when deciding whether to pass or rush. . Scarlett plays as a power play quarterback, as a key defenseman on the penalty kill, and everything in between, giving him invaluable experience, something he also gained playing for Canada-Pacific in the U17, and Canada for the U18's.

Scarlett's glaring weakness comes in his strength, particularly in the upper body area. Scarlett has trouble with some of the stronger oncoming forwards, and can get knocked around, or overpowered in these situations, no matter how good his positioning is. Because he is 6'1" 165 pounds, it will take him 2+ years to be effective at both ends of the ice against men. Reece will be looked at as a project. However, with all the skill Scarlett has, he is a project who will likely go somewhere in the second round, as his upside is still solid, and considering his main flaws are easily worked out, and can be taken care of in junior, his value is still high. Just don't expect him to make the jump to the NHL right away.

Cody McNaughton

RW – Guelph, (OHL)
Born Oct 16 1992 - Petawawa, ONT
Height 5.10 - Weight 180 - Shoots R

DRAFT GUIDE' 11

Games	Goals	Assists	Points	PIMS	+/-
68	15	21	36	122	-9

Cody is a former 1st round selection by the Guelph Storm. McNaughton was a star player on the powerhouse Toronto Jr.Canadiens 1992 team. He hit everything that moved and showed great scoring ability to go along with it. We loved the pick when Guelph grabbed him in the first round. So what happened? Well for starters he has not got taller since minor midget. He hasn't developed offensively as expected, but plays with that same ton of energy, and drive he played with every shift on the Canadiens. Cody is an effective penalty killer, with an outstanding compete level. He has decent positioning in the offensive zone, and could be found very valuable by a team looking for a high energy forward in the later rounds. McNaughton had a great playoff before getting suspended for a questionable hit. Cody could be that great story down the road of that player that took the long route but made it.

Phil Hudon

RW – Choate-Rosemary, (HS USA)
Born April 15, 1993 -Montreal, QC
Height 6.00 Weight 190 - Shoots R

DRAFT GUIDE' 11

Games	Goals	Assists	Points	PIMS	+/-
22	10	10	20	24	NA

The Montreal product who has been playing his hockey south of the border in U.S prep school hockey will be an interesting player to watch come draft day. Hudon is a winger with decent size and ability. His hands are above average and he has no glaring skating issues. His speed is pretty good and he moves around with decent quickness for his size. His work ethic is fairly solid, he shows good battle skills along the walls and fighting for position in front of the net. There is not an overly large body of work for scouts to get a read on Hudon. The prep school schedule is a far cry from that of a major junior schedule. Competition is also a step below which is always a challenge for scouts when trying to project what a player is capable of at higher levels of hockey. Hudon has no glaring weaknesses and when you watch him he comes across as a pretty impressive prospect. Our only red flag would be the lack of huge offensive numbers posted at this level. Having said that, numbers can be misleading at the best of times. We see Hudon somewhere in the 3rd round range.

Zack Mitchell

RW – Guelph Storm (OHL)
Born Jan 7 1993 - Caledon, ONT
Height 6.00 -- Weight 174 - Shoots R

Games	Goals	Assists	Points	PIMS	+/-
39	5	21	26	80	+4

Mitchell was selected by the Guelph Storm in the 4th round of the 2009 OHL Priority Selection. Mitchell has always shown good skill and work ethic, but in his rookie season it appeared he would have a rough time getting picked in the NHL draft due to his size. After seemingly falling off the map to the scouting world, Mitchell has noticeably grown, and has excelled in an expanded role given to him by the Storm. He now plays all game situations, including the penalty kill where he has proven to be fairly valuable. Offensively Zack found his stride later on in the season putting up 16 points in his final 23 games (including playoffs) this also included 3 goals in his last 4 games of the season. Mitchell had more than a point per game in the playoffs for Guelph as his role expanded further. With Guelph losing several players, Mitchell will get top minutes for the Storm, and will likely be counted on as heavily on the power play, as he is on the penalty kill. An NHL team could likely take him late, because it appears he is only going to get better.

Nikita Kucherov

RW - CSKA 2, RUSSIA-JR.
Born June 17, 1993
Height 5.10 - Weight 163 - Shoots R

Games	Goals	Assists	Points	PIMS	+/-
41	27	31	58	81	NA

Nikita made quite a statement at the U18's in Germany. He lit up the scoreboard over and over while taking away some of the spotlight from his teammates, Grigorenko and Yakupov. Who are far from chop liver. The young Russian is not a huge kid but he has amazing speed and scoring ability. He has a good burst and jumps on pucks quickly. His shot is a laser and is accurate. Sounds great right? He's a lock for the first round right? Not so fast. Kucherov is the Forrest Gump box of chocolates, you never know what you're going to get with him. Will the player who can score with anyone in the draft show up or will he mail in half his shifts? We will tell you right now that this player could get drafted anywhere from around the early 20's on. We plugged him in after the 2nd round due to the risk associated with this player. Nikita has a 1st round talent grade by us. Where to draft him is up for debate.

Zachery Franko

DRAFT GUIDE' 11

LW – Kelowna Rockets (WHL)
Born Mar 9 1993 - Winnipeg, MAN
Height 5.10 Weight 160 Shoots L

Games	Goals	Assists	Points	PIMS	+/-
72	22	31	53	22	8

Originally committed to Bemidji State, Franko got more ice as the season rolled along in Kelowna and made good use of it. He had a very solid World Under 17 in Timmins in 2010 where he first hit HockeyProspect.com's radar. Franko has proven he can put the puck in the net at the WHL level. He is a bit light in the size category but continues to get a bit bigger. The shifty forward had a strong January which seemed to grab him some attention. No longer flying under the radar Zach has now been noticed by the scouting community. Zach' Skating is good. He has outstanding speed and he is a smart hockey player who can be very creative in the offensive zone. Franko has great offensive skills. Regardless of possible size issues, this is a kid we like. Zach is responsible player all over the ice but lacks strength for battles along walls.

Scott Oke

DRAFT GUIDE' 11

RW – St.John Sea Dogs (QMHL)
Born Mar 16 1993 - St-Lambert, PQ
Height 6.02 Weight 185 Shoots L

Games	Goals	Assists	Points	PIMS	+/-
54	5	5	10	15	+3

Oke's point production has really been down, but he may just be having a problem adjusting his game to the 4th line. He's no grinder and his game is more about puck-controlling than about dump-and-chase. He has really good abilities one-on-one and a very good release on his wrist shot which is really tough for goalies to handle. He has a smooth skating style, not really explosive though, but he is good at finding open ice. He should try to shoot more often as he tends to wait a couple of seconds too long before making his decision, shooting or passing. Defensively, he's got to work harder on the boards with his big frame. He needs to shield the puck with his body better and chip pucks out more often rather than making poor turnovers. When the confidence is there, it's going to be easier to make the nifty breakouts. He needs to add some strength.

Adam Clendening

Defense – Boston University (NCAA)
Born Oct 26 1992 - Wheatfield, NY
Height 5.11 - Weight - 190 - Shoots R

Games	Goals	Assists	Points	PIMS	+/-
39	5	21	26	80	+4

Clendening was an invitee to the NHL Research camp in Toronto back in August and struggled a bit in front of the huge number of NHL scouts. The Boston University freshman saw his stock drop this season. It was not all that long ago that you heard Clendening and 'first rounder' mentioned in the same breath. We have watched Adam going back to his GTHL days and saw potential but feel he has a ways to go to be seen as a first round talent. Adam is sub 6'0 which always makes things a bit tougher if you are a defenseman. While he moves the puck pretty well and shows some smarts, his skating is not at the elite level. Clendening boasts an impressive resume and seems to be a real competitor. He can be put in the category of a winner as he has recently enjoyed multiple gold medals as a member of team USA. Adam's only recent 'failure' to speak of was being cut from the USA World Junior team that took part in Buffalo this past holiday season.

Ryan Tesink

C - Saint John Sea Dogs (QMJHL)
Born May 21 1993 - Saint John, NB
Height 6.00 - Weight 161 - Shoots L

Games	Goals	Assists	Points	PIMS	+/-
59	8	27	35	38	+26

Tesink is young 17 year old that should have been on a higher line than the 4th line, but with the talent in Saint-John, he has been on the 4th line for the majority of the season. He is a pretty skinny 6'0" player but he plays the game with loads of energy. He has a good nose for the net and he creates a lot of space with the cycling game as he his very dynamic and speedy. He needs to add muscle to his frame in order to win more 1-on-1 battles and be more effective with the body. Ryan progressed pretty well during the season as he was mostly running around on the ice in the first months of the season. Now he has settled down to play a more intelligent game. It has helped him get more scoring chances. Tesink improved leaps and bounds as far as being a better player in all 3 zones.

Brent Andrews

LW – Halifax Mooseheads (QMJHL)
Born Jan 19 1993 - Hunter River, PEI
Height 6.02 - Weight 200 - Shoots L

Games	Goals	Assists	Points	PIMS	+/-
68	12	17	29	33	-22

Andrews has really fallen in the draft rankings because of the poor work ethic he put into his games. He has the tools to become a good-to-great player, but lack of intensity and confidence has really made him struggle throughout the majority of the season. Andrews is a big kid but he doesn't throw his weight around too often as far as laying the body goes. He does use his size pretty well to win battles and protect the puck. He uses his frame and quick moves to get into the slot, but he doesn't hit the net enough. He hangs on the puck too long and gives time for the defensive players to setup. He glides too much in the defensive zone to be effective and he doesn't use his body enough to cut down chances. He is a real horse. He doesn't lose a whole lot of 1-on-1 and body positioning battles. He needs more explosiveness in the neutral zone. With more hard work, improved confidence and less thinking, he could become a heck of a player.

Sean Kuraly

Center - Indiana Ice (USHL)
Born Jan 20 1993 - Dublin, OH
Height 6.02 - Weight 192- Shoots L

Games	Goals	Assists	Points	PIMS	+/-
51	8	21	29	45	+5

Kuraly has the prototypical power forward frame. He was extremely impressive at the USHL Fall Classic, a preseason showcase for the league. Kuraly continued his great play throughout the regular season as well. He has a nose for the puck, and is not afraid to fight for it. He uses his big frame to his advantage, out muscling defenseman to the puck. If he goes into the corner, a good bet is to say Kuraly's coming out with the puck. He gives equal effort at both ends of the ice, earning him a lot of time on Indiana's penalty kill, and ended up tied for the lead in short-handed goals in the USHL this year. Kuraly battles in front of the net, using his height to screen goaltenders and gain offensive opportunities for his team. His offensive potential has not yet been reached as it has never really been a focus of his game. He's got a lot of pro potential as long as he can start putting the puck in the net more often, combining his great size with offensive skill.

Joseph Labate

Center - Holy Angels (HS USA)
Born May 2 1992 Burnsville, MN
Height 6.04 - Weight 180 Shoots L

Games	Goals	Assists	Points	PIMS	+/-
25	27	22	49	42	NA

Labate would not be known for his defensive abilities at this point in his career. He is all offense. The 6-4, 180 pounder needs to gain a level of consistency in his game. He can look a bit lazy at times and can drive scouts and coaches crazy with how good he can look one shift and then not so much on the next shift. Much like another high school power forward from last year, Nick Bjugstad, Labate has some pretty large upside to him. He has a knack for banging home stuff around the net. His skating is good and will only get better as he gets stronger. As an example, Boone Jenner added quite a bit of power to his stride this season and it did wonders for his overall game. The basics on this kid are that he can score, has an NHL frame, and is not all that big on playing defense just yet. Both his effort and Dzone coverage is a mess. He is a raw prospect with a pretty big upside. Labate is headed to the Wisconsin Badgers.

Robbie Russo

Defense - USNTDP (HS USA)
Born Feb 15 1993 - Westmont, IL
Height 6.00- Weight 190 - Shoots R

Games	Goals	Assists	Points	PIMS	+/-
52	3	19	22	23	NA

Russo, a stay at home defenseman, who impressed at the 2010 Fall Classic. He makes great decisions and is one of the most consistent defenseman coming out of the USHL this year. Robbie is a very skilled defender who handles the puck well and is the Q.B on the powerplay. Russo anticipates passes and is quick to get on a knee and or uses an active stick to block passes. He usually forces the puck handler to take a bad shot from the outside. Russo also kills penalties and is a mature and poised player all over the ice. Robbie has committed to play his NCAA hockey at Notre Dame. Russo is a very solid hockey player and an overall sound defenseman. We rank him as a player with large upside and a good overall NHL prospect.

Nick Shore

Center - U. of Denver (NCAA)
Born Sep 26 1992 - Denver, CO
Height 6.00 - Weight 195 - Shoots R

DRAFT GUIDE' 11

Games	Goals	Assists	Points	PIMS	+/-
28	7	11	18	14	NA

Shore is a solid two-way forward. He has very good hockey sense and we love the fact that he makes good decisions with the puck. Nick has very good hands and plays a smart game distributing the puck. Shore is a freshman this year at Denver where he has had a fine season. He uses his size pretty well and does a great job of protecting the puck. He is probably a pass first guy but he can put the puck in the net. He would have plenty more goals if he just used his great shot more often. We love this kid's grit and overall work ethic on each shift. He is a player any coach would want on his team and would rely on in any situation.

Adam Lowry

LW - Swift Current Broncos (WHL)
Born Mar 29 1993 - St. Louis, MO
Height 6.04 - Weight 186 - Shoots L

DRAFT GUIDE' 11

Games	Goals	Assists	Points	PIMS	+/-
66	18	27	45	84	-21

Adam Lowry was selected in the 4th Round of the 2008 WHL Bantam draft by the Swift Current Broncos. Adam, the son of former NHLer Dave Lowry, has tremendous size to work with. Lowry was expected to put up big points after having a solid rookie season; however, he only put up slight improvements statistically from a year ago. Adam is very effective in the corners, and takes pride in winning battles, and fighting for pucks both in the corners, and along the boards at both ends of the ice. Lowry is a respectable skater for 6'4", has a decent shot, and decent hands. Lowry needs to hit the weights and get bigger, as he has a big frame that still needs to fill out quite a bit. Next season should be interesting for Adam, as he is going to be expected to take on an even bigger role with Swift Current. The Broncos are expected to lose at least 4 forwards from this past season, and Lowry will once again be looked towards to add to his point totals. Mono caused him to lose weight and miss the full month of September.

Maximilien Le Sieur

RW - Shawinigan Cataractes (QMJHL)
Born Sep 27 1992 - Westmount, PQ
Height 6.02 - Weight 203 - Shoots R

Games	Goals	Assists	Points	PIMS	+/-
68	16	28	44	37	+7

Le Sieur is another big body in Shawinigan, with his 6'0" 203 pound frame. It's all about winning battles with the 18 years old forward from the Shawinigan Cataractes. He isn't flashy but he plays a pretty effective north-south board game with a nice scoring touch around the net. Rarely do you see him cause turnovers in the offensive zone. He is good at bringing the puck to the net. He uses his body well to take opponents out of play. He is solid at jumping on rebounds, fore-checking and passing the puck to the front of the net. You don't always notice him much during games, but he plays a rather simple game. He makes space for his teammates and he's willing to sacrifice his body night after night. He needs a bit more fine tuning in his game. He needs to get better at handling the puck, gain more explosiveness and get quicker in his D-Zone coverage. You know what you are going to get game after game with Le Sieur.

Travis Ewanyk

LW - Edmonton Oil Kings (WHL)
Born Mar 29 1993 - St. Albert, ALTA
Height 6.01 - Weight 178 - Shoots L

Games	Goals	Assists	Points	PIMS	+/-
72	11	16	27	126	-3

Travis Ewanyk was selected in the 3rd round of the 2008 WHL Bantam Draft, and was brought up quickly by Edmonton, despite not earning a ton of ice time. Despite being under 6 feet tall and 168lbs at this time last season, Travis is nearly 6'1" and 190 pounds, which has done wonders for his game. Ewanyk is a low risk player, who plays with a ton of heart, drive and determination. Travis will contribute offensively at times, and has done so very well, but his future is largely placed around the grinder ability he shows. Travis executes this game so well, that we feel there's very little risk that he will become a very good bottom 6 forward at the NHL level. We feel it's a little more unlikely that he will be a regular in the top 6 at the NHL level. Travis is a fan favorite in Edmonton, and leads by example. We were impressed with his work ethic during the season, playoffs, and at the World Under 18 Championship in Germany. Travis is excellent in the faceoff circle which gives him yet another tool towards becoming an NHL regular.

Gabriel Beaupré

Defense – Val D'Or (QMJHL)
Born Nov 23 1992 - Chrysostome, PQ
Height 6.02 - Weight 195 - Shoots L

Games	Goals	Assists	Points	PIMS	+/-
66	3	15	18	73	-27

Gabriel Beaupre is a defensive D-man with offensive potential, but he has smarts all over the ice, which puts him ahead of others. He plays a physical game, he's a strong kid and he wins most of his battles along the boards. He can get pretty tough without taking penalties. His stick positioning is always good; he is willing to put his body in front of every puck that he can get to. He blocks a lot of shots and never gives up on any play. He gives 2nd effort to recover for a teammate's mistake and he never puts himself in a position where he is vulnerable. We think he has more offensive potential than his stats show. He has good mobility but adding some explosiveness to his game would help him. He has a good shot, but he needs to have more confidence in it to contribute more.

Josh Currie

LW - P EI Rocket (QMJHL)
Born Oct 29, 92 - Charlottetown, PEI
Height 5.10 - Weight 170 - Shoots R

Games	Goals	Assists	Points	PIMS	+/-
52	9	11	20	9	-3

An energy winger, he puts maximum effort in every zone on the ice. He was a 3rd line player for the majority of the season on a defensively driven team. As a result his point production hasn't been that great, but he has good tools. A tremendous penalty killer, he blocks a lot of shots and he is a pretty effective forechecker. He's not the hardest hitter, but the pressure he is able to put in the offensive zone, particularly on the defenseman, can cause many turnovers. He has good speed and an active stick to cut passing lanes. He handles the puck pretty well and he has some pretty slick moves. He needs to work on the release of his shot, particularly when he needs to let it go in tight areas. We like the energy he brings on the ice as he never stops working, and he is a tempo setter for his team. He's not the most creative player or the most talented, but he plays an effective north-south, dump-and-chase game.

Anton Zlobin

LW - Shawinigan Cataractes (QMJHL)
Born Feb 22 1993 - Moscow, Russia
Height 6.00 - Weight 187 - Shoots R

Games	Goals	Assists	Points	PIMS	+/-
59	23	22	45	28	+10

The young Russian forward took a while before adapting correctly to the North American game, but now that he's confident on the ice, he has progressed. Zlobin has a lethal wrist shot and he likes to change direction quickly, get in the slot, and let his shot go. He can create offense at high speed. He positions well in the offensive zone to score goals, he knows where to be and he doesn't need a whole lot of space to score goals. Like most Russian players, Anton handles the puck well, and he doesn't shy away from physical contact although he rarely initiates it. He has a good work ethic and his defensive play got better as the season went along. He needs more speed in his game, more strength to win his battles and more experience in his zone. He's a nice project as he has come miles from where he was at the beginning of the season.

Artem Sergeev

Defense - Val d'Or Foreurs (QMJHL)
Born Apr 20 1993
Height 6.01 - Weight 205 - Shoots L

Games	Goals	Assists	Points	PIMS	+/-
64	5	22	27	40	-13

A Russian defenseman, playing a North American game, Sergeev uses a strong physical presence on the boards and a booming slap shot to make himself noticed coming into the 2011 NHL Draft. He likes to use his big frame to be pretty aggressive and get the check on the opponent. He can get caught trying to be too aggressive and he doesn't have the skating ability to recover fast enough. But with the strength he has, he is effective at checking and pinning opponents on the boards when his timing to contain is on. He needs to stay more focused on his positioning in the defensive zone. He makes a really good tape-to-tape first pass, has good puck protection and soft hands. His slap shot is really good. It's a pro caliber shot and he can really be a good weapon on any powerplay.

Mitch Elliot

LW – Seattle Thunderbirds (WHL)
Born July 15, 1993 Prince George, BC
Height 6.05- Weight 215 Shoots L

Games	Goals	Assists	Points	PIMS	+/-
72	5	8	13	118	-27

Elliot is a physical machine that finishes his checks whenever possible, and does so with authority. Mitch plays an energy line role with Seattle, and works hard every shift, showing off good skating, which is really something that is exceptional for someone who measures in at 6'5"plus. Elliot is an effective fighter, and plays his role to perfection, winning battles along the boards, and making life difficult for any opposing player in his path. Mitch handles the puck a limited amount of times in a game, but when he does, he makes the smart play either passing it off to a more skilled linemate, or will dump the puck in deep, and chase it. He will occasionally take a pointless penalty, but considering the depth of the draft, we should see this big man, who could turn into an excellent bottom six player taken in the mid rounds of this year's draft.

Zac Larraza

Center - USANTDP (USHL)
Born Feb 25 1993 - Scottsdale, AZ
Height 6.02 - Weight 192 - Shoots L

Games	Goals	Assists	Points	PIMS	+/-
49	8	5	13	20	NA

This is a bit of a tough player to figure out. If you see him for the first time he has a very big wow factor to him. A huge kid with pretty good hands and he is a really nice looking skater. The more we saw Zac, the more we struggled to figure out why he can't put more points up on the board. We love this kid's compete level. What he seems to lack in high end scoring skills, he makes up for with heart and energy. He is a pretty smart player in his own zone. He has a good commitment to the defensive side of the game. Zac works hard on the forecheck and reads the play pretty well in the neutral zone. He seems to stay pretty loyal to the systems employed by his coaches. Larraza has many tools that NHL teams love to see. He is an excellent skater with a very solid stride. His first few steps are really good for anyone, let alone a big kid. Throw in a power forward frame and you get the general picture. Put a checkmark in the possible 'dark horse' department.

Brennan Serville

Defense – Stouffville Spirit, (OJHL)
Born Jun 2 1993 Pickering, ONT
Height 6.02 - Weight 184 – Shoots R

DRAFT GUIDE' 11

Games	Goals	Assists	Points	PIMS	+/-
36	3	27	30	29	NA

Serville was drafted by the Sudbury Wolves in 2009 but decided to return to the Stouffville Spirit again this season. Serville recently committed to the University of Michigan and has competed on Team Canada East as well. Serville is as a great skater who moves the puck well with a good quick first pass. His decision making is very good as he makes good choices with and without the puck all over the ice. He would probably best be described as a two-way defenseman. We like his high hockey IQ and fantastic skating ability. Serville has improved his play on the powerplay. He makes better decisions with the puck while with the man advantage and has improved his shot as well. The upside is there for this kid. His skating is already great and will only get better as he gains more strength in his legs. He needs to work hard in the gym to get physically stronger all over to assist him in those board battles.

Phil Di Giuseppe

LW - Villanova Knights (OJHL)
Born Oct 9 1993 Maple, ONT
Height 6.01 - Weight 200 - L

DRAFT GUIDE' 11

Games	Goals	Assists	Points	PIMS	+/-
49	24	39	63	25	NA

Di Giuseppe, a Niagara Ice Dogs draft pick is a player we know pretty well. Phil played a weekend for an HP prospects team and also was a player that HP founder Mark Edwards helped recruit to the Villanova Knights. Phil is excellent along the walls, he has really quick feet and is elusive and hard to pin. He protects the puck well and has a quick burst off the walls driving to the slot. He is more of a goal scorer than a playmaker but he has come quite a ways in improving his play in that area. Di Giuseppe is a good skater with very good hands. He slowly learned to protect the puck off the rush and has made things happen since he made this change. Phil's shot is very good and is pretty accurate. We have seen him score some highlight real goals that show of his scoring ability. Phil needs to work on his upper body strength. This will surely happen next season when he reports to the University of Michigan. While not ranked by NHL Central Scouting, we think at minimum that Phil could be a very solid late round pick.

Matt MacLeod

LW – Brampton Battalion (OHL)
Born Jul 13 1993 -- Niagara Falls, ONT
Height 6.01 -- Weight 181 -- Shoots R

Games	Goals	Assists	Points	PIMS	+/-
52	5	8	13	34	-7

Brampton's second pick in the 2009 OHL priority draft, MacLeod needs to play in the power forward mold. He has yet to put up top numbers in the OHL, and if drafted, it will be based on his potential. He posted points in Minor Midget. If he doesn't develop top 6 scoring potential, MacLeod will need to perfect a power forward style game to crack a pro roster. MacLeod will need more time at the OHL level to develop. We would like to see a bit better decision making in his game.

Frankie Corrado

Defense – Sudbury Wolves (OHL)
Born Mar 26 1993 -- Woodbridge, ONT
Height 6.00 -- Weight 188 -- Shoots R

Games	Goals	Assists	Points	PIMS	+/-
67	4	26	30	94	-10

Corrado can really skate. He has shown the ability to go coast to coast, and put up some numbers this season for Sudbury. The goal scoring ability he showed when the Wolves drafted him has eluded him at the OHL level. He has 5 goals in 134 games. While he can wow you at times, we feel that Corrado will need to find his scoring touch and develop a more consistent defensive game to have a chance to become an NHL defenseman.

Michael Curtis

LW – Belleville Bulls (OHL)
Born Jan 26 1993 -- Mississauga, ONT
Height 6.00 -- Weight 185 -- Shoots L

Games	Goals	Assists	Points	PIMS	+/-
58	9	9	18	32	-25

Skating in his second season for Belleville, Curtis has shown a lot of tools, but needs to put it together into a consistent package. There is no doubt he can really fire the puck (which is his most outstanding skill), but his decision making in when to apply that skill has left Hockey Prospect's scouts flustered. He can kill penalties and plays a well-rounded game that could be valuable on the bottom six of an NHL squad.

Adam Reid

LW – USA U-18 (USHL)
Born Jan 29 1993 -- Chino Hills, CA
Height 6.04 -- Weight 205 Shoots L

Games	Goals	Assists	Points	PIMS	+/-
44	9	6	15	33	+1

The big left winger has power forward size and great hands, a deadly combination. Consistency is a bit of an issue here, but that should improve with time and experience. He has a great shot that overpowers USHL goalies. A big issue that drops Reid's value a bit is skating, as with many large prospects it can be an issue. If he can improve his skating weaknesses, he becomes a much better NHL prospect.

Brady Austin

Defense – Erie Otters (OHL)
Born Jun 16 1993 -- Bobcaygeon, ONT
Height 6.04 -- Weight 230 -- Shoots L

Games	Goals	Assists	Points	PIMS	+/-
59	1	12	13	47	10

Brady Austin recently completed his second season with the Erie Otters of the OHL. He has a big frame coupled with toughness that could translate well to the NHL. He will never stand out as the flashiest player on the ice, but is not offensively inept. Should Austin continue to progress, get stronger, and remain willing to drop the gloves, he could turn into a tough, stay at home defenseman.

Max Everson

Defense – Edina High, (HS USA)
Born February 22, 1993 -- Edina, MN, USA
Height 6.00 -- Weight 184 Shoots L

Games	Goals	Assists	Points	PIMS	+/-
22	4	17	21	20	NA

Everson is one of those defensemen that you may leave the game without noticing. Max is a smart player who seems to make all the right plays all over the ice. He plays a simple game but is impressive. He does not seem to excel in any one area, tools seem average in all facets. One of those steady Eddy guys who just goes about his business and gets the job done.

Barclay Goodrow

LW – Brampton Battalion (OHL)
Born Feb 26 1993 -- Aurora, ONT
Height 6.02 -- Weight 209 -- Shoots L

Games	Goals	Assists	Points	PIMS	+/-
65	24	15	39	36	-4

Goodrow has the size and skill set to play pro hockey. He needs to develop his battle skills along the boards. Nonetheless, the size is there, and he can put the puck in the net. Goodrow could turn into a dominant force next year at the OHL level, if he commits himself to playing a true power forwards game. His development in that area will determine if his game transforms him into a player who will make a real run at an NHL roster down the road.

Justin Sefton

Defense – Sudbury Wolves (OHL)
Born May 2 1992 Prince George, BC
Height 6.03 Weight 199 Shoots R

Games	Goals	Assists	Points	PIMS	+/-
66	5	6	11	124	-8

Sefton is a prime example of a D-man with tools, but hasn't put it all together yet to warrant a high pick. He has a nice booming shot that he can control, and he is willing to fight. We would like to see Sefton make better decisions all over the ice. His skating may still hold him back in the long run. His feet are a little heavy and have hindered his progress thus far in his OHL career.

Jesse Forsberg

Defense – Prince George Cougars (WHL)
Born Aug 13 1993 -- Waldheim, SASK
Height 6.00 -- Weight 194 -- Shoots L

Games	Goals	Assists	Points	PIMS	+/-
57	2	14	16	144	+4

Jesse Forsberg is a former 11th overall pick in the WHL Bantam Draft. Forsberg is a tenacious player who really battles hard along the walls and just hates to lose battles. He is a tough kid with a willingness to drop the gloves. Jesse has fallen as far as draft stock goes but still hangs in there as a potential draft pick for some team. He will need to play a bit smarter going forward in his career and make better decisions. As we mentioned in last season's guide, Forsberg's hunched over skating style does not help his cause at all.

Frank Palazzese

G – Kingston Frontenacs (OHL)
Born May 28 1993 -- Mississauga, ONT
Height 6.01 -- Weight 165 -- Catches L

Games	Wins	Losses	G.A.A	Save %	SO
34	7	16	4.16	.890	0

Featured in the Hockey Prospect 2011 Prospect Preview book, Palazzese played a solid amount of games in net for Kingston this year. His numbers were not fantastic, but he has a strong developing skill set. We are still fans of Palazzese. Goalies develop so much slower and Frank had a pretty solid finish to his regular season. Frank is an athletic kid who has the tools to make his mark in the OHL going forward.

Joshua Leivo

LW – Sudbury Wolves (OHL)
Born May 26 1993 -- Innisfil, ONT
Height 6.02 -- Weight 180 -- Shoots R

Games	Goals	Assists	Points	PIMS	+/-
64	13	17	30	37	-10

On a rather weak Sudbury team, Leivo had a relentless motor on the forecheck. He has good size, and his style of play translates well to the NHL. He could be the type of player that doesn't put up numbers as good as other draftees, but his style of play makes it quite possible for him to find a role on the bottom 6 of a team down the road in his career.

Petr Beranek

RW – Barrie Colts (OHL)
Born Jul 8 1993 -- Brno, Czech Rep.
Height 6.01 -- Weight 199 -- Shoots R

Games	Goals	Assists	Points	PIMS	+/-
54	11	15	26	22	-12

Playing his first season in North America, Beranek came from the Czech Republic with a his nice resume. He doesn't have great speed, but skates well and has a solid offensive skill set. Whether or not Beranek will be a pro player will be much easier to forecast based on his performance in his second season at the OHL level.

Jordan Auld

Defense – Brampton Battalion (OHL)
Born Jan 16 1993 -- Toronto, ONT
Height 6.02 -- Weight 195 -- Shoots R

Games	Goals	Assists	Points	PIMS	+/-
62	1	16	17	20	-12

Auld came off a strong season with his Telus Cup silver medalist Midget AAA Mississauga Reps to join Brampton this season. He had a relatively solid season in his first year at the major junior level. Auld has a nice offensive set, good passing ability and is a solid skater. To take his game to the next level, Auld has to continue to learn the mental aspect of playing defense, and work on his quickness.

Dylan Smoskowitz

Center – Barrie Colts (OHL)
Born Feb 11 1993 -- Richmond Hill, ONT
Height 6.00 -- Weight 175

Games	Goals	Assists	Points	PIMS	+/-
67	21	10	31	44	-18

Dylan played a few games on the HP summer league team and showed off his skills. Smoskowitz has a high ceiling. He plays hard, and was able to crack the 20 goal plateau this season. He knows where to go on the ice to score goals, and if he can get stronger and improve his skating, he has a shot at improving his chances to sign a pro contract. We really feel that improvement in strength and his play along the walls will be a key factor for his success going forward.

Brayden Rose

Defense – Owen Sound Attack (OHL)
Born Jan 29 1993 -- Richmond Hill, ONT
Height 5.11 -- Weight 186

Games	Goals	Assists	Points	PIMS	+/-
45	2	6	8	67	+12

An HP favorite, as he is an entertaining player to watch. Rose is a tough, physical defenseman for Owen Sound. He played a solid role for what was a powerhouse Owen Sound team. He is a pretty simple player to watch: physical along the boards, not much offensively, and willing to stand up for his teammates. He would likely play the same role in the NHL if he continues to develop his game.

Tyler Graovac

Center – Ottawa 67's (OHL)
Born Apr 27 1993 -- Brampton, ONT
Height 6.02 -- Weight 180 -- Shoots R

Games	Goals	Assists	Points	PIMS	+/-
66	10	11	21	10	-4

Graovac is the prototypical 3 zone player. He is fun to root for as he works his tail off in the defensive zone and around the boards. On top of the hard work, he put up some numbers this year for Ottawa. He sometimes looks like a 3rd defenseman out there, and, if he is going to crack the NHL, it will likely be in a checking/penalty killing role. We like his up-side, he was very good in some of our viewings.

Cameron Brace

RW – Owen Sound (OHL)
Born Apr 8 1993 -- Toronto, ONT
Height 5.10 -- Weight 165 -- Shoots R

Games	Goals	Assists	Points	PIMS	+/-
61	11	6	17	62	-1

Brace did not get as much playing time as perhaps he expected this season on a stacked Owen Sound squad, but did well considering his limited role. He is undersized, but is a fantastic skater and has the stick to finish his chances. He needs to get much stronger, without sacrificing his skating to advance to the next level. Next season, with more playing time following a strong playoff run, Brace may show more of the numbers he is capable of posting in the OHL

Steven Janes

RW – Ottawa 67's (OHL)
Born Feb 24 1993 -- Etobicoke, ONT
Height 6.02 -- Weight 180 -- Shoots L

Games	Goals	Assists	Points	PIMS	+/-
17	4	2	6	13	0

Janes is a power forward project who has come miles in his development over the last two seasons. He has the size but will need to keep improving his skating. He is going to have to add scoring touch to his game if he is going to jump to the professional level. However, he has the on-ice drive to be effective. Injuries limited Janes to only 17 games plus playoffs this season.

Jacob Riley

G – Sudbury Wolves (OHL)
Born Mar 18 1993 -- London, ONT
Height 6.00 -- Weight 165 -- Catches L

Games	Wins	Losses	G.A.A	Save %	SO
31	7	11	3.52	.895	0

Started his season off in Brampton before being traded to Sudbury, Riley is a still developing netminder. He has good size, athletic ability, and can recover, but has to work on staying compact in net, and not over commit. It will be interesting to see what he does as a true starter at the OHL level. Flashes of greatness but as with many young goalies, weak goals plagued him.

Nick Foglia

RW/C – Ottawa 67's (OHL)
Born Mar 28 1993 -- Brampton, ONT
Height 5.10 -- Weight 185 -- Shoots R

Games	Goals	Assists	Points	PIMS	+/-
67	4	8	12	22	-8

Nick was a player we really liked in minor midget because of his tireless work ethic. Foglia has not grown much since then though and may be a bit undersized for the NHL given his lack of point totals. He plays hard and chippy. His skating is fantastic, he has blazing speed and can kill penalties He has never been much of a scorer, but if he gets a little bigger, he may be able to become an energy guy at the NHL level. Nick has always been a very smart hockey player.

Tyson Teichmann

G – Belleville Bulls (OHL)
Born May 19 1993 -- Belleville, ONT
Height 6.00 -- Weight 150 -- Catches L

Games	Wins	Losses	G.A.A	Save %	SO
42	11	26	4.22	.880	1

Teichmann entered the season high on various lists as a top prospect. We had him ranked behind several OHL goalies including Binnington, Mahalak and Palazzese and nothing has changed for us. Teichmann has good reflexes and athletic ability, but has to work on his positioning, and fix some mental lapses within games. He is going to need to hold off Malcolm Subban (2012 Draft) as the starter for Belleville next season to move his career in a positive direction.

Matthew Mahalak

G – Plymouth Whalers (OHL)
Born Jan 22 1993 -- Monroe, MI
Height 6.02 -- Weight 185

Games	Wins	Losses	G.A.A	Save %	SO
20	7	12	3.20	.902	1

One of the more intriguing goalie prospects this year. Mahalak is an American born goaltender that suited up for Plymouth this season. He played the backup role, but played it well after a very slow start. Matt improved his save % from .848 in December all the way up over the .900 threshold by years end. He started to look like the highly touted goalie he entered the league as. If he performs as well next season, Mahalak might end up being a steal if taken in the mid-rounds of the draft.

Colten St. Clair

Center – Fargo, (USHL)
Born November 22, 1992 Chandler, AZ, USA
Height 5.10 Weight 190 Shoots R

Games	Goals	Assists	Points	PIMS	+/-
42	11	14	25	25	+6

We see limited upside with this forward who suits up for Fargo in the USHL. St. Clair is a bit of a work in progress. He works hard but has limited upside as far as transferable NHL skills are concerned. Colten is limited by a lack of real scoring ability and the fact that he is slightly under the size foot mark. He is not tiny, but based on his lack of elite skills you would want him to be slightly bigger to fill the role of a crasher and banger at the NHL level.

Brian Bunnett

RW – Wellington Dukes (OJHL)
Born Apr 21 1993 -- Bowmanville, ONT
Height 6.01 -- Weight 190

Games	Goals	Assists	Points	PIMS	+/-
49	16	17	33	26	NA

Bunnett has a big frame. This baby face kid has plenty of room to fill out. Decent skater but is an area where improvement is needed. Brian has very good hands and a hard accurate shot. He is very smart with the puck. He makes good decisions and uses his teammates well. He needs to play a bit bigger and make sure he wins all his battles along the walls. Lots of upside if his skating develops. Having solid playoffs and on his way to a possible RBC Cup with the Dukes.

Austin Wuthrich

LW – USA U-18, (USHL)
Born Aug 11 1993 -- Anchorage, AK
Height 6.02 -- Weight 185 - Shoots R

Games	Goals	Assists	Points	PIMS	+/-
5	1	1	2	2	NA

Despite suffering a broken leg this season, forward Austin Wuthrich has secured a scholarship and will attend Notre Dame. A big forward who needs to prove he is over the injury. Limited Viewing due to injury.

Michael Paliotta

Defense – USA U-18, (USHL)
Born Apr 16 1993 -- Westport, CT
Height 6.03 -- Weight 198 - Shoots R

Games	Goals	Assists	Points	PIMS	+/-
52	1	12	13	71	NA

Another big prospect from the USNTDP. Paliotta uses his size to his advantage. He seems to love contact, especially in front of the net, clearing the crease for his goaltender. This love for contact can get him into some trouble with the referees however. His decision making ability could use some improvement, keeping his physicality in check in certain situations. His stock dropped slightly in second half of the season.

Brian Ferlin

LW – Indiana, USHL
Born Jun 3 1992 -- Jacksonville, FL
Height 6.01 -- Weight 196

Games	Goals	Assists	Points	PIMS	+/-
55	25	48	73	26	+26

Another second year eligible player, Ferlin has made significant improvement from last season. Third in the USHL in scoring this year, Ferlin benefited from playing on Indiana's first line, which made up for all three of the top three in USHL scoring. Next year he needs to prove that this season was not just a fluke and that he is a legitimate NHL prospect.

Andy Welinski

Defense – Green Bay Gamblers (USHL)
Born April 27, 1993, Duluth, MN
Height 6.00 Weight 188 -Shoots R

Games	Goals	Assists	Points	PIMS	+/-
51	6	8	14	14	+10

The Gambler's second best scoring defenseman played well in his first season in the USHL. We'd like to see him play more consistently, making better decisions in the defensive zone. When he gets offensive chances at the point, he usually takes them and converts them into offensive opportunities for his team. He is right on track with his development and another year or two in the USHL should be good for him.

Brendan Woods

Defense – Muskegon, (USHL)
Born Jun 11 1992 -- Palmyra, PA
Height 6.02 -- Weight 190 - Shoots L

Games	Goals	Assists	Points	PIMS	+/-
57	14	12	26	86	-10

Muskegon's Woods, a second year eligible player was snubbed in last year's draft because of an arm injury early in the season. From last year to this year, Woods has made constant improvements, and is a very good power forward for the Lumberjacks. Woods needs to improve more on the offensive side of the puck to be a complete player, but the physical tools are all there.

Curtis Leonard

Defense – Wellington Dukes (OJHL)
Born Sep 23 1992 -- Napanee, ONT
Height 6.03 -- Weight 200 – Shoots L

Games	Goals	Assists	Points	PIMS	+/-
48	2	20	22	20	NA

Curtis has a pretty big frame but needs to fill it out more. He has some good tools and logs tons of minutes for the Dukes who at this writing are heading to the RBC Championship. Needs to improve his pivots a bit and show a bit more poise with the puck. Leonard makes some bad plays with the puck when under heavy forecheck that leads to turnovers. His overall toolset is pretty good and he plays in every situation for his team.

Josiah Didier

Defense – Cedar Rapids, USHL
Born Apr 8 1993 -- Littleton, CO
Height 6.02 -- Weight 200 Shoots R

Games	Goals	Assists	Points	PIMS	+/-
59	8	13	21	81	+5

Didier is a jack-of-all trades for the RoughRiders. He can play a physical game at times, and can also jump in on the rush when needed. He does need improvement on both sides of the puck, but he has plenty of potential both ways. Josh is definitely a project player that could very well turn into a solid two-way defenseman in the future.

Blake Pietila

RW – USA U-18, USHL
Born Feb 20 1993 -- Brighton, MI
Height 5.11 -- Weight 189 - Shoots L

Games	Goals	Assists	Points	PIMS	+/-
52	13	9	22	51	NA

Blake is a sub 6'0" speedster with limited scoring skills. Blake is a pretty smart player who creates his scoring chances through smarts and hustle. We love this kids work ethic and willingness to battle. Blake has a willingness to commit to the defensive side of the puck. Pietila is a player who will need to showcase the strong parts of his game as he continues to develop in the NCAA with Northern Michigan. His overall game and good hockey IQ should warrant a selection in or around the 4th round.

Jordan Ruby

G – Wellington Dukes (OJHL)
Born Feb 22 1991 -- Tavistock, ONT
Height 6.01 -- Weight 189 Catches L

Games	Wins	Losses	G.A.A	Save %	SO
35	26	5	2.21	.932	3

Ruby is in his second season with the Dukes after turning down various CHL offers. He has chosen to go the NCAA route. The big goaltender has suited up for Team Canada East and performed quite well. Ruby is very quick post to post and makes himself big in the net. His rebound control is good and he is very athletic. One slight weakness might be some inconsistency with his glove hand. At this writing Ruby is about to take part in the Dudley Hewitt Cup.

Dan Carlson

Defense – USA U-18, USHL
Born May 14 1993 -- Corcoran, MN
Height 6.01 -- Weight 201 – Shoots L

Games	Goals	Assists	Points	PIMS	+/-
50	3	5	38	42	1

A very defensive minded forward, Carlson makes a nice bottom six grinder. He doesn't give up on plays, and does his best to create offensive opportunities for his team. Carlson loves contact, constantly playing the body instead of the puck. He consistently makes the highlight reels with checks along the boards. Dan is destined to be a solid presence on the third or fourth line.

Reid Boucher

Defense – USA U-18, (USHL)
Born Sep 8 1993 -- Grand Ledge, MI
Height 5.10 -- Weight 192 Shoots L

Games	Goals	Assists	Points	PIMS	+/-
49	24	19	43	25	NA

Reid is not a very big kid but still has a baby face and might just grow some more. He is a pure goal scorer and he has a bit of an "it" factor to him. Boucher needs a ton of work in his own zone. He is committed to Michigan State, and is a very skilled offensive threat, whose assets are definitely his hands and shot. He needs to improve his speed to become a very explosive player. He needs to develop more of a physical side to his game to compliment his offensive skills. He is a player we will be interested to see when he gets drafted in June.

Austin Czarnik

Center – Green Bay, (USHL)
Born Dec 12 1992 -- Washington, MI
Height 5.08 -- Weight 140 Shoots R

Games	Goals	Assists	Points	PIMS	+/-
46	20	14	34	33	+2

A center out of Washington, Michigan, Czarnik is a talented goal scorer whose skill is overshadowed by his size. Czarnik is a player who helps his team by scoring clutch goals in the third period. His size is what is holding him back. He has a great offensive talent, but durability is a big issue with a player of his size.

Jay Williams

G – Waterloo, USHL
Born Jun 7 1993 -- McLean, VA
Height 6.01 -- Weight 170 Catches L

Games	Wins	Losses	G.A.A	Save %	SO
20	7	10	3.49	.891	2

Jay was one of our top ranked goalies two years ago when we scouted him for the OHL Draft. We loved Williams back when we scouted him with the TPH Thunder. We saw Williams in Rochester last summer and after a bit of a rough year 2009/2010 he got it going a bit in Rochester and has bounced back this season. Williams is a big kid who moves well in his net. He is agile and has a high compete level. He is able to steal games on occasion and has shown no glaring weaknesses. We like his chances to keep raising his stock.

Garrett Haar

RW – Fargo, (USHL)
Born Aug 16 1993 -- Huntington Beach, CA
Height 5.11 -- Weight 190

Games	Goals	Assists	Points	PIMS	+/-
51	7	16	23	38	+9

Haar is a talented power forward coming out of Fargo. He uses his body to his advantage, playing a very confident style of hockey. He needs to start putting up more points. Haar is more of a playmaker than a finisher in the offensive zone, and he could stand to improve his shot accuracy to start picking his corners and scoring more goals.

Michael Houser

G – London Knights (OHL)
Born Sep 13 1992 -- Wexford, PA
Height 6.01 -- Weight 185 -- Catches L

Games	Wins	Losses	G.A.A	Save %	SO
54	30	19	3.32	.904	1

Houser was easily London's most valuable player this season. Without this kid in net we are positive that London would have missed the playoffs and would have a top 4 pick in this year's OHL Draft. We had Houser ranked in last year's draft guide and he was passed over. We don't expect him to be passed over again this season. Compete level and athleticism are off the charts. His ability to recover quickly and make second and third saves is unreal. Rebound control improved.

Matej Machovsky

G – Brampton Battlion (OHL)
Born Jul 25 1993 - Opava, Czech Rep.
Height 6.02 -- Weight 191 -- Catches L

Games	Wins	Losses	G.A.A	Save %	SO
23	7	13	2.90	.904	1

Started the season with the Guelph Storm but was traded to Brampton to open up an import spot for incoming Richard Panik. We were lucky and were present at the Powerade Centre for many of Matej's starts. In our opinion, he the best goaltender on the Battalion. We liked his lateral quickness and the way he challenged shooters. Like any young goalie his rebound control is a work in progress but it's not bad. His glove hand and athletic ability are solid. We really like this goalie and expect him to really come into his own next season.

Zach Saar

RW - Chicago, (USHL)
Born Jun 22 1993 -- Plainwell, MI
Height 6.04 -- Weight 190 - Shoots

Games	Goals	Assists	Points	PIMS	+/-
32	4	6	10	38	-20

A big right winger off the Steel, Saar is an interesting prospect to read. He's got great size, that's for sure. His skills are very raw and he could make for a great project player. His role, unlike most NHL prospects, hasn't been totally determined yet. He will probably end up being a bottom six power forward or grinder, but if placed in the right situation with the right coaches, Saar could develop his offensive skills exponentially.

Aaron Harstad

Defense – Green Bay, (USHL)
Born Apr 27 1992 -- Stevens Point, WI
Height 6.02 -- Weight 200 - Shoots L

Games	Goals	Assists	Points	PIMS	+/-
51	7	14	21	73	+17

Harstad is 6'2" 200 lbs and plays a more defensive-based game than offensive. However, he does have some skills to help put numbers on the board. Harstad shone offensively in Wisconsin High School hockey, averaging two points a game. He plays the body well and almost always finishes his checks. He lacks a bit in the area of blocking shots and taking away passing lanes.

Maxime Lagacé

G – PEI Rocket (QMHL)
Born Jan 12 1993 -- Saint-Augustin, PQ
Height 6.02 -- Weight 177 – Catches L

Games	Wins	Losses	GAA	Save%	SO
18	8	4	3.59	.884	1

Maxime didn't play a whole lot this season behind Evan Mosher, one of the best goalies in the league. Lagacé follows the play really well. He has good positioning and pucks through screens tend to hit him. He is pretty aggressive, he likes to poke check near his net. He needs to mature. Sometimes he can look unconfident and shaky when giving up a bad goal or making a bad play. His quickness and agility in front of his net is great. With more seasoning, he's going to be one of the top goalies in the Q.

Max Friberg

LW – Skovde, (SWEDEN-3)
Born November 20, 1992-- Skovde, SWE
Height 5.11 -- Weight 185 Shoots R

Games	Goals	Assists	Points	PIMS	+/-
34	13	27	40	6	NA

Max has some very basic tools that make him an NHL prospect but he is a real longshot to make the league. Skating is a weakness and we question many aspects of his game including a questionable work ethic. Max did not really show us anything more than average ratings in any aspect of his game. We didn't find him to be a player with a high level hockey IQ. He made far too many poor decisions.

Zachary Yuen

Defense – Tri-City Americans (WHL)
Born Mar 3 1993 -- Vancouver, BC
Height 6.00 -- Weight 205 -- Shoots L

Games	Goals	Assists	Points	PIMS	+/-
72	8	24	32	65	+41

Yuen was the final selection in the first round of the 2008 WHL Bantam draft by the Tri-City Americans. Yuen is a two-way defenseman who is an effective skater, and has very good size and strength. Yuen can rush the puck up the ice fairly well when he so choses, and can throw decent hits although not overly physical. Yuen is a reliable defenseman who is effective in all game situations, but never seems to try to do too much.

Colin Smith

Center – Kamloops, (WHL)
Born Jun 20 1993 -- Edmonton, ALTA
Height 5.10 -- Weight 162 -- Shoots R

Games	Goals	Assists	Points	PIMS	+/-
72	21	29	50	61	-21

What he lacks in size he makes up for in smarts, speed and heart. A recent member of Canada's U18 team, Smith had a solid tournament in Germany. He has quick feet and moves well in small spaces. Not shockingly he struggles against bigger opponents and is tested in one on one battles. He uses a good hockey IQ and the ability to read the ice quickly to get the most out of his talent. He is not quite as willing to mix it up in the dirty areas as some of the other smaller forwards in the draft.

Miikka Salomaki

RW – Karpat, FINLAND
Born Mar 9 1993 -- Raahe, Finland
Height 5.11 -- Weight 195 -- Shoots L

Games	Goals	Assists	Points	PIMS	+/-
40	4	6	10	53	+2

Could Salomaki be the second coming of Sami Pahlsson? He certainly seems to play a similar style. Miikka made the jump to the SM-liiga despite only being 17. He put up respectable points, but was particularly impressive with the compete level he showed regularly. Salomaki is a solid skater, and will need some time before he comes over, but could be a solid energetic player.

Patrick Koudys

Defense – RPI (NCAA)
Born Nov 15 1992 -- Hamilton, ON
Height 6.02 -- Weight 190 -- Shoots L

Games	Goals	Assists	Points	PIMS	+/-
32	1	2	3	14	NA

We have watched this player for quite a few years now going back to Junior B and his time with the Burlington Cougars. He has good size and moves well. He played a very simple stay at home game this year at RPI but we did see some offensive upside in his game previous to his freshman year in the NCAA. Patrick has solid tools and size and is worth drafting in the mid rounds.

Samuel Windle

Defense – Des Moines, (USHL)
Born Mar 10 1992 -- Maple Grove, MN
Height 6.04 --Weight 200 Shoots-R

Games	Goals	Assists	Points	PIMS	+/-
58	6	10	16	27	0

Windle's a big defenseman who stepped into the USHL this season and shoved his weight around. Not really the offensive minded player, Windle is a "one trick pony", being a lockdown defenseman. He still needs to skate with a wider base, getting more leverage on his opponents. Adding a bit more of an offensive side to his game would only help.

Max McCormick

Center – Sioux City, (USHL)
Born May 1 1992 -- De Pere, WI
Height 5.11 -- Weight 175 – Shoots L

Games	Goals	Assists	Points	PIMS	+/-
55	21	21	42	102	+6

Playing on the Musketeers' first line, McCormick went from unknown to a leading scorer for the Sioux City squad. He needs to improve all facets of his game, but he does have potential left in the tank. He's got a solid offensive skill set to build off of. This is a feisty player who is not afraid to drop the gloves and play a rough and tumble game. He has a pretty quick right hand too!

Mike Pereira

LW – U. Mass., (NCAA)
Born Nov 24 1991 -- West Haven, CT
Height 5.11 -- Weight 170 -- Shoots L

Games	Goals	Assists	Points	PIMS	+/-
32	12	13	25	22	NA

Pereira is an interesting prospect. He shows some flashy skills and speed and scored an impressive 12 goals as a freshman this year for U Mass. We would like to see him round out his game by being more creative and showing a better work ethic in the defensive part of his game. He has shown scouts he can score, but did he shown enough to sell scouts that he can earn ice at the NHL level? He is not a huge kid so he will need to continue to work on all aspects of his game.

Robert Steeves

G – Acadie-Bathurst, (QMJHL)
Born Jan 19 1993 -- Moncton, NB
Height 5.11 -- Weight 155 – Catches R

Games	Wins	Losses	GAA	Save %	SO
21	11	5	2.67	.914	3

Robert never gives up on any play and he's one of the quickest goalies in the league. His lateral movement and rebound control is high end. He follows the play very well and he has good focus. even in heavy traffic he keeps calm. He's a bit of a project for any team taking him at the draft as He needs to put on some pounds, polish his play around the net, and get a bit better positioning wise on his angles. He has all the tools it takes to be a great goalie, mental toughness and raw talent.

Gabriel Bourret

Defense – Saint John, (QMJHL)
Born Oct 9 1992 -- Laprairie, PQ
Height 6.00 -- Weight 173 -- Shoots R

Games	Goals	Assists	Points	PIMS	+/-
63	8	25	33	72	+26

Bourret has shown flashes of brilliance and flashes of play that would make scouts move on to the next prospect. Bourret has decent size and can chip in on offense from the back end. He has average feet and does not shy away from contact. Bourret has shown a willingness to drop the gloves when needed. He is a mid-level prospect who has upside as a tough competitor who has shown an ability to post points at the QMJHL level.

Gustav Bjorklund

Center – Vasteras Jr., (SWE-JR.)
Born Feb 23 1993 -- Stockholm, SWE
Height 5.08 -- Weight 152 -- Shoots R

Games	Goals	Assists	Points	PIMS	+/-
34	20	21	41	77	NA

Gustav Bjorklund finished strong leading Sweden's U18 team in points. Bjorklund played for Vasteras U20, putting up big points, and saw some time with the men's league team. Bjorklund is a very quick skater with strong acceleration and a solid top speed. He has good hands in close, and is willing to get into the slot area. He is not timid against contact from bigger players despite his size. He has a great shot with a solid release. Gustav can get knocked around occasionally.

Samuel Henley

LW – Lewiston, (QMJHL)
Born Jul 25 1993 -- Val-d'Or, PQ
Height 6.04 -- Weight 195 -- Shoots L

Games	Goals	Assists	Points	PIMS	+/-
63	13	18	31	37	+13

It's tough to have impressive numbers considering that he's playing on the 3rd line in Lewiston and getting no powerplay time. Henley is 6'4" 195 lbs, and has very good hockey sense. His defensive zone game is pretty good, he doesn't turn over the puck often, and is solid getting pucks out safely along the wall. Offensively, more creativity would be nice to see. We think he has more talent than his statistics show. He plays the role of a 3rd line player right now, grinding down low, being physical on opposing D's and putting pressure around the net for rebounds.

Colin Sullivan

Center – Avon Old Farms, (HS USA)
Born March 26, 1993 -- Milford, CT, USA
Height 6.00 -- Weight 190 -- Shoots R

Games	Goals	Assists	Points	PIMS	+/-
27	3	12	15	14	NA

Sullivan is an outstanding skater and it's the first thing you notice about him after watching a few shifts. He has complete control of his edges and is able to handle rushing forwards very well. He plays a pretty simple game. We would like to see him take advantage of his skating and become more of a puck moving offensive player. He didn't show us a real grasp for the position in a puck moving capacity. He didn't make great decisions with the puck and rushed plays too often. More poise is needed to bring him to the next level.

Keegan Lowe

Defense – Edmonton, (WHL)
Born Mar 29 1993 -- Edmonton, ALTA
Height 6.01 -- Weight 173 -- Shoots L

Games	Goals	Assists	Points	PIMS	+/-
71	2	22	24	123	+33

Keegan is the son of former Edmonton Oilers defenseman Kevin Lowe. Keegan was selected in the 6th round by the Oil Kings, and has emerged as a very good pick in that round. Keegan does a little bit of everything, but not too much of anything. He is a smart defender, who is willing to play physical and drop the gloves. He doesn't have a ton of offensive upside, but where his future lies is in the heart and soul type of play he has exhibited throughout this season.

Mike Reilly

Defense – Shattuck-St. Mary's, (HS USA)
Born July 13, 1993 -- Chicago, IL, USA
Height 5.10 -- Weight 150 -- Shoots L

Games	Goals	Assists	Points	PIMS	+/-
48	13	30	43	26	NA

There is much to like about Reilly but will he ever grow? The 5'10" 150 pound defenseman has an uphill battle ahead of him to gain the size needed to reach the NHL. Mike plays a smart game and does just about everything well. He moves the puck smartly and understands how to play defense. The physical side of the game is a challenge. Reilly is the classic case of risk reward based on size concerns. Reilly is a solid defenseman with good offensive upside. Reilly would be a good risk late in the draft.

Steven Fogarty

RW – Edina High, (HIGH-MN)
Born Apr 19 1993 -- Edina, MN
Height 6.02 -- Weight 195

Games	Goals	Assists	Points	PIMS	+/-
24	23	17	40	12	NA

Fogarty played all season in High School hockey before jumping to the Chicago Steel of the USHL to get a taste before seasons end. Fogarty is far from a great skater but he is a big kid who plays a solid overall brand of hockey. He is great along the walls and dishes out some physical play. Although skating is not a huge strength, his hands are very good. He likes to park his big frame in front of the net and bang home rebounds. He is pretty adept at it and an interesting prospect.

Keevin Cutting

Defense – Owen Sound Attack (OHL)
Born Sep 22 1992 -- Bracebridge, ONT
Height 6.01 -- Weight 177 -- Shoots R

Games	Goals	Assists	Points	PIMS	+/-
68	2	14	16	61	+23

Cutting skates well and possesses pretty good speed and agility. He struggles with defensive zone coverage and decision making in his own end. He does throw his weight around nicely. He could be better with his passing accuracy. Cutting needs to mature as a player and eliminate unforced errors from his game. Cutting's size and skating ability make him an attractive package with some upside. We just see mistakes too often. He might hang on to a top 210 spot.

Samuel Noreau

Defense – Baie Comeau, QMJHL
Born Jan 31 1993 -- Montreal, PQ
Height 6.04 -- Weight 206 -- Shoots R

Games	Goals	Assists	Points	PIMS	+/-
67	5	5	10	141	-13

Noreau is probably one of the most feared players in the league and he is only 17 years old. He's 6'4" 206 pounds, tough, mean, but not dirty. He does not hit to injure. He needs to work on his mobility. He has progressed nicely in his decision making this season. He's taking fewer risks and not playing overly aggressive. Certain times emotions take over, but with maturity Noreau's going to be a better player. He needs to work on his puck skills and his passing. We saw him fight more than 10 times and he's a fighter to notice.

Markus Granlund

Center – HIFK JR., (FINLAND-JR)
Born Apr 16 1993 -- Oulu, Finland
Height 5.10 -- Weight 169 -- Shoots L

Games	Goals	Assists	Points	PIMS	+/-
40	20	32	52	49	NA

Markus is the younger brother of Mikael Granlund, the Top 10 pick in last year's draft by the Minnesota Wild. Markus isn't quite as talented, but is skilled playmaker. He was the captain and a top point producer for Finland in the U18's surpassed only by Joel Armia. Granlund has great hands and decent skating ability. Due to his size we expect him to still be a few years away, as he is likely to play in the SM-liiga full time next year for HIFK.

Dillon Donnelly

Defense – Shawinigan, (QMJHL)
Born Sep 7 1993 -- Amherst, NY
Height 6.02 -- Weight 193 -- Shoots L

Games	Goals	Assists	Points	PIMS	+/-
63	1	7	8	153	-10

Donnelly is a player who might exceed some expectations when all is said and done. He has great size and although he does not jump off the ice at you when you watch him, he impressed us in our viewings. The former first round pick of the Moncton Wildcats is a tough physical defenseman. Dillon has the ability to drop the gloves and flashes a pretty quick and powerful right hand. Donnelly needs plenty of development but did surprise us with his decent hands. Decision making can be an issue at times. Donnelly has enough to get a good look by NHL teams.

Aidan Kelly

Center – Saint John, (QMJHL)
Born Feb 15 1993 -- Saint John, NB
Height 6.01 -- Weight 189 -- Shoots L

Games	Goals	Assists	Points	PIMS	+/-
49	6	4	10	22	+3

Kelly is another young Saint John player fighting his way into getting enough ice time to show-case his talent. Kelly put up points in minor hockey and has shown flashes of that skill at the QMJHL level. We like his overall game and work ethic. He shows a pretty good hockey IQ and buys into his role. The issue with Kelly is his skating. While it has improved, it's the biggest fac-tor relating to where he will end up being selected this June.

Dylan Wruck

RW – Edmonton, (WHL)
Born Sep 23 1992 -- Saskatoon, SASK
Height 5.08 -- Weight 162 -- Shoots L

Games	Goals	Assists	Points	PIMS	+/-
71	38	40	78	44	+25

It's always fun scouting the little guys. We were high on Tyler Ennis and others in recent drafts. There is no debate about Wruck's skill level. We love his heart. He shows no fear going to dirty areas and plays bigger than his size. Our problem with Dylan is that we are not sure he is even as big as his listed size. While height is one issue, weight is another. We really think that Wruck will struggle with certain aspects of the game given his weight. We see him as a possible flier pick.

Sam Grist

RW – Tri-City, (WHL)
Born Jun 27 1993 -- N. Saanich, BC
Height 6.04 -- Weight 210 -- Shoots L

Games	Goals	Assists	Points	PIMS	+/-
56	0	3	3	107	-11

Grist is a huge defenseman, who joined the Tri-City Americans after spending last year in the BCHL with Victoria. Grist is not exactly known for his offensive upside, but is known for his physical play and ability to punish opposing players. Grist plays a fairly simple game, and is will-ing to stand up for teammates, and drop the gloves when needed.

Nikita Nesterov

Defense – Chelyabinsk 2, RUSSIA-JR.
Born March 28, 1993 -- Russia
Height 6.00 -- Weight 183 Shoots R

Games	Goals	Assists	Points	PIMS	+/-
46	5	14	19	72	NA

Nesterov was selected 16th overall in the CHL Import Draft by the Tri-City Americans of the WHL last year, as well as going in the 1st round of the KHL Draft by Traktor Chelyabinsk. It is unknown what path Nesterov will choose going into next season; however, he spent last year in the MHL. Nesterov is a two way defenseman, who likes to play physical and can rack up the PIM's. He is also is a good skater who shows great positioning on the power play, and has a great point shot.

Nick Malysa

Defense – Plymouth Whalers (OHL)
Born Apr 11 1993 -- Bridgewater, NJ
Height 6.00 -- Weight 193 -- Shoots L

Games	Goals	Assists	Points	PIMS	+/-
65	1	9	10	102	+11

Malysa, a 5th Round selection by Plymouth in 2009, has been a developing member of the Whalers' blueline. Sometimes Malysa is a player who you need to look for to really notice. A low risk/low reward defenseman who has respectable size at this point. Nick is a stay at home defenseman, with decent positioning, and has a good physical element to his game.

Matt McNeely

G – USA U-18, (USHL)
Born Feb 16 1993 -- Burnsville, MN
Height 6.02 -- Weight 205- Catches L

Games	Wins	Losses	G.A.A	Save %	SO
25	9	12	3.82	.893	0

The backup tender to the highly touted John Gibson probably doesn't get enough praise for his abilities. Much like Gibson, Matt has good size and solid technique. He is in the shadows this season but it's not uncommon for goalies that get drafted as backups to wind up being steals in the draft. McNeely moves well and does everything at a high enough level right now to warrant being selected with a mid-round selection.

Destry Straight

Center – Coquitlam, BCHL
Born March 22, 1993-- Vancouver, BC
Height 6.00 -- Weight 163 Shoots L

Games	Goals	Assists	Points	PIMS	+/-
59	26	41	67	48	NA

Straight is a very skilled forward who needs to get stronger and increase his willingness to mix it up a bit more in the dirty areas. Destry is going to be headed to Boston College in the fall of 2012. Straight needs to put the puck in the net in order to keep his value to his team high. He is not a star in his own end. Destry may get drafted based on his offensive talent and potential.

Craig Duininck

Defense – Windsor, (OHL)
Born Apr 29 1993 -- St. Cloud, MN
Height 6.01 -- Weight 200 -- Shoots R

Games	Goals	Assists	Points	PIMS	+/-
66	7	15	22	65	NA

Duininck was selected 4th Round by Windsor out of Detroit Compuware. He had an effective rookie season, and was expected to break out this season, however didn't reach expectations. Craig has great size, and has decent skating. He plays a two-way game that leans more towards defensive play. He has shown the ability to be very physical, but will make some mental mistakes.

Harrison Ruopp

Defense – Prince Albert Raiders (WHL)
Born Mar 17 1993 -- Zehner, SASK
Height 6.02 -- Weight 198 -- Shoots R

Games	Goals	Assists	Points	PIMS	+/-
54	0	9	9	98	+8

Ruopp was selected by Prince Albert in the 2008 WHL Bantam Draft. Ruopp went in and out of the line-up the last two years. He is a very defensive minded defenseman, who gets a lot of his points from moving the puck out of the zone, more than anything. Ruopp is extremely physical, has great size, and doesn't hesitate to impose his will. Ruopp was one of HP's under-the-radar guys, but judging by his late season popularity, the secret is out about Harrison Ruopp.

Viktor Arvidsson

LW – Skelleftea Jr. (SWE-JR)
Born April 8, 1993 -- Skelleftea, SWE
Height 5.08 -- Weight 165 -Shoots R

Games	Goals	Assists	Points	PIMS	+/-
40	15	19	34	51	NA

Arvidsson's season started with Skelleftea's U18 team; however, after putting up 14 points in 4 games, Arvidsson was moved to the U20. Viktor is an extremely strong skater, who is very quick and elusive. He can make some outstanding moves 1 on 1, and despite not putting up big points in the U18 tournament, made a big impression with his show of skill and speed.

William Karlsson

Center – Vasteras Jr., (SWE-JR)
Born January 8, 1993 -- Marsta, SWE
Height 6.00 -- Weight 163- Shoots Left

Games	Goals	Assists	Points	PIMS	+/-
38	20	34	54	45	NA

Karlsson spent most of his time with Vasteras in between the U20 team, and the men's team who currently competes in the Allsvenskan league. Karlsson proved to be one of Sweden's key offensive contributors mirroring forward Victor Rask's production. Karlsson showed off his great skating ability, combined with his physical play. Karlsson plays at a very high energy, but is also very creative, and has the ability to make high difficulty passes under pressure.

Colby Drost

G – New England Huskies (EJHL)
Born Jan 21, 1992 -- Franklin Lakes NJ
Height 6.01 -- Weight 195- Catches L

Games	Wins	Losses	G.A.A	Save %	SO
33	10	18	3.69	.904	0

For the second year in a row we include Drost. Last year we told you he should have been drafted out of Holderness Prep. This year Colby stood on his head for a bad Huskies team. We told some OHL and QMJHL teams about him last June. We expect him to sign with a QMJHL team and be ready next fall. Colby is a competitor. He is a big kid who is very quick and directs rebounds very well. His skating is solid. He is technically sound, keeps getting better and should be drafted.

Zakhar Arzamastsev

Defense – Novokuznetsk, (RUSSIA)
Born November 6, 1992-- Russia
Height 6.02 -- Weight 205 -Shoots L

DRAFT GUIDE' 11

Games	Goals	Assists	Points	PIMS	+/-
47	3	5	8	6	NA

Arzamastsev checks in at 6'2" 205 lbs, and is actually a fairly mobile defenseman. Arzamastsev has great size and uses it appropriately. He played full time with Metallurg Novokuznetsk. Arzamastsev has good hands, and can make the simple play with the puck and may have some intriguing upside. His stock falls partially due to the fact that he's under contract to the KHL until 2013-2014.

Johan Sundstrom

Center – Frolunda, (SWE)
Born September 21, 1992 -- Gothenburg, SWE
Height 6.02 -- Weight 196 Shoots Right

DRAFT GUIDE' 11

Games	Goals	Assists	Points	PIMS	+/-
41	1	0	1	10	NA

Sundstrom has some upside as a big kid that is capable of playing the Center position. Johan didn't jump out at us but the more we watched the more we could see little things in his game that made him valuable. He played smart and seemed to always be in position. His work ethic impressed us as he worked hard in all three zones. In the end, Sundstrom will need to address his skating, as he has no burst and an ugly stride. He has shifts where he really looks slow.

Rasmus Bengtsson

Defense – Rogle, (SWEDEN-2)
Born May 14, 1993-- Landskrona, SWE
Height 6.02 -- Weight 189 Shoots L

DRAFT GUIDE' 11

Games	Goals	Assists	Points	PIMS	+/-
45	2	7	9	6	NA

Rasmus is a pretty good puck moving defenseman who makes accurate passes and good decisions on where he should move the puck. He has good agility and shows good gap control on 1 on 1's. Bengtsson showed a good awareness of when to pivot, and has a good burst getting to his man closing the gap and playing him smartly along walls. He showed a bit of offensive upside and we saw him unleash some pretty fast moving pucks from the blueline.

Tyler Hansen

Defense – Kamloops, (WHL)
Born Mar 17 1993 -- Magrath, ALTA
Height 6.02 -- Weight 192 -- Shoots R

Games	Goals	Assists	Points	PIMS	+/-
59	8	13	21	81	+5

Hansen was drafted in the 3rd round by the Kamloops Blazers, Hansen has taken over a fairly important role with the Blazers throughout this season. He plays a good physical game, throwing hard, clean hits, but also maintains solid defensive positioning. Hansen was used quite often on the penalty kill as well. He has very limited offensive upside.

Maxim Shalunov

RW – Chelyabinsk 2, (RUSSIA-JR.)
Born January 31, 1993--Chelyabinsk, RUS
Height 6.03 -- Weight 185 Shoots Left

Games	Goals	Assists	Points	PIMS	+/-
39	22	14	36	42	NA

In 2010 Shalunov was selected by Traktor Chelyabinsk 15th overall in the KHL Draft. He made an appearance there after playing most of the season in the MHL. Shalunov played in the U-18 after just turning 17, posting 4 points. Then he returned this year, putting up a similar performance. Shalunov combines great size, puck handling abilities, and skating to be an impactful player. At times Shalunov will choose not to work, or show any effort which is frustrating.

Tadeas Galansky

G – Saginaw, (OHL)
Born Dec 29 1992 -- Brno, Czech Rep.
Height 6.03 -- Weight 189 -- Catches L

Games	Wins	Losses	G.A.A	Save %	SO
17	9	5	2.89	.910	1

Galansky was selected 33rd overall in the 2009 CHL Import Draft by the Saginaw Spirit. Galansky has served very well for the Spirit as a back-up goaltender the last two seasons. Due to his strong size, Galansky covers the lower part of the net very effectively, and his angles are very strong. Tadeas will be expected to take over the starting role in Saginaw. He has been eased in nicely, and we expect him to put together a very solid season.

Dylan Willick

RW – Kamloops, (WHL)
Born October 19, 1992-- Prince George, BC
Height 5.10 -- Weight 184 -- Shoots R

Games	Goals	Assists	Points	PIMS	+/-
72	24	20	44	53	-17

Willick is kid we really like. He is one of those players that coaches can count on. He is great on the penalty kill and plays smart hockey. He has very good speed and is a hard working forward. Although not huge, Dylan does not shy away from contact. He wins battles and competes all over the ice. He has good agility and his shot is good. Willick is a player with a good knowledge of what is expected of him. He might be looked back on as a steal in this draft.

Dillon Simpson

Defense – North Dakota, (NCAA)
Born Feb 10 1993 -- Edmonton, ALTA
Height 6.00 -- Weight 192 -- Shoots L

Games	Goals	Assists	Points	PIMS	+/-
27	2	8	10	6	NA

This was not exactly the season that Simpson was looking for in his NHL Draft season. As the son of former NHL'er Craig Simpson and nephew of Dave Simpson, Dillon has NHL bloodlines. Simpson has enough size to make it to the next level but probably lacks a bit in the skating department right now. Simpson had trouble getting enough ice time to make a huge impact this season. He shows the smarts you would expect from a former NHL'ers son. Simpson has not done enough to be a high pick but will surely be snatched up on draft day.

Zach Hall

Center – Barrie, (OHL)
Born Apr 29 1993 -- Belleville, ONT
Height 5.11 -- Weight 170 -- Shoots L

Games	Goals	Assists	Points	PIMS	+/-
38	8	4	12	9	-24

Hall is an HP dark horse player. We saw Hall play often last year in the OJHL where he lit the league up as a rookie with 71 points in 44 games with the Couchiching Terriers. Hall was impressive during his call up games last year with Barrie as well. This year coming back from injury he clawed his way in to getting ice time. Hall has great offensive talent and we would not be surprised to see a big improvement in his numbers next season if he is healthy.

Nathan Lieuwen

Goalie – Kootenay, (WHL)
Born Aug 8 1991 -- Abbotsford, BC
Height 6.05 -- Weight 192 -- Catches L

Games	Wins	Losses	G.A.A	Save %	SO
55	33	16	2.79	.903	3

A nice story here as the 1991 born goaltender has had a fantastic year and has forced himself into the draft picture. Lieuwen was a highly touted tender in his draft year in 08/09 but struggled a bit with injuries and a less than stellar .885 save percentage. When you are a 6'5" goaltender who posts the numbers that Lieuwen has posted this season, NHL teams will take notice. NHL teams love these big tenders that can move well. Nathan is very quick and has no glaring weaknesses.

Jeremy Boyce

LW – Timra, (SWEDEN)
Born August 28, 1993-- Stockholm, SWE
Height 6.00 -- Weight 170 -- Shoots L

Games	Goals	Assists	Points	PIMS	+/-
33	1	2	3	4	NA

Boyce could end up being a steal for some NHL team depending on where he winds up being selected in June. The speedy Boyce is capable of putting pucks in the net. He plays smart and understands the game in all three zones He is able to read plays and move into position to score very well. We would like to see him commit to all areas of the game more consistently. He can show lazy shifts and lack of effort at times. We love his upside and skating won't hold him back as it is high end.

Albin Blomkvist

Defense – Linkoping Jr., (SWE-JR)
Born Jan 8, 1993 -- Kristianstad, SWE
Height 6.03 -- Weight 196 -- Shoots L

Games	Goals	Assists	Points	PIMS	+/-
26	0	5	5	85	NA

Albin was a player who jumped out at us during the U 18 in Germany. Blomkvist played a big, tough game and we detected a bit of a mean streak. He made very good passes in all three zones. He played smart and had a good grasp of his position. He did a nice job of erasing opposition forwards along the walls. We thought his shot looked good but he didn't show it off enough. He seemed to be a player that was more focused on the defensive part of the game.

2

Player Interviews

Dan Catenacci
Center – Soo Greyhounds
Conducted March, 2011

HP: Could you just give a quick assessment of what's gone on in Sue St. Marie this year with the team

Daniel: I think, starting off from the beginning we went through a lot of injuries here, and we also have something like 12 rookies on the team so we have a lot of first year guys. It's been tough not having that veteran presence. You know we're not going to make the playoffs, but for the remaining 5 games, the guys just want to play for pride and play for each other.

HP: With all the rookies, guys like yourself, who might only be in their second year, or even like your Captain who has been asked to step up in the leadership role. Have you gotten into that, have you been a leader and a mentor? How has that helped you off the ice?

Daniel: My coach at the beginning of the year picked me as an assistant captain, and I was honored to be one. I think me, along with Brock and the other assistants have done a pretty good job this year, so far. You can't really say that the team's success, this year, is based on our leadership. I think it's been tough with all the first year players and I think also games have been really close this year. It's the little things that have hurt us over and over. Sometimes you can't really explain a loss or something like that. It's been a really weird season for our team. I haven't been through something like this before.

HP: It's definitely a new experience and something you experienced last year was the whole OHL priority draft being drafted first overall by Sue St. Marie Greyhounds. I'm sure Sue St. Marie was a brand new experience for you. It's kind of a secluded franchise. When I talk to fans they say they treat you guys as the Toronto Maple Leafs of the OHL – very high standards. When you found out all this, what was going through your mind, knowing that, hey I'm first overall, so I've got the expectations on my back, the team is closely watched. Have you been through that type of pressure before?

Daniel: I think every top pick in the OHL draft kind of went through that pressure, going through that in minor midget. When I first came to the Soo, I saw my face of the front page of the paper.

You're kinda like, wow you're 16, you're not really used to that. You know in Sue St. Marie they really support their hockey team. As I found out this year, it's tough to play here when you're not doing well. The fans are really great, they're always really supportive. But once again it's been a really tough year this year, I think dealing with the pressures. I think last year I kinda had a tough time dealing with the pressure of being first overall. I think this year I came in with a new mindset, didn't worry about it, and just played my game.

HP: Growing is part of it all and this season you had a tale of two seasons so to speak, maybe

even three. I'm going to run down the stats. I'm sure you're sick of hearing this. 18 goals, 37 points in 29 games to start the year. Then of course you had the lull, where you had 3 goals, 21 points in 26 games. And now you've gotten back on track with 5 or 6 goals, and 10 points in the last 4 or 5 games. Three different stretches, what can you say about those or maybe why it happened.

Daniel: I started off the season really good, and heading into the Christmas break. After Christmas I kind of had a little bit of slump. Honestly, I can't really describe it. I play one of my best games and came out of it without a point. You know, so many crossbars, and missed nets and stupid stuff like that. You can't really get down on yourself. Obviously you start to lose confidence. I think the reason I got out of it was I just kept shooting and keeping it simple. Staying positive I think was the biggest thing.

HP: One thing you got to not be frustrated about was your time at the top prospects game. You guys were in there early. I think you had 3 or 4 days in the ACC, taking it all in. From the skills competition to the end of the game you were highlighted. Can you talk about your short-handed goal in the top prospects game?

Daniel: I honestly thought the other team scored on that play before - it was downright rushed. As soon as the puck flew out there I saw a defenseman fall. I knew I could beat the __. I skated all the way down I gave a little fake and put it five hole. It's kind of one of those things you don't even think about you just do it. I was really excited after that.

HP: Doing a little research, I came across a video of yourself for a try-on skate weight. Basically, a commercial you were starring in. The main focus of that particular product is to increase your speed. You have too much of it I would say. Speed is a huge part of your game. How does one train with all that speed or was it just naturally gifted to you?

Daniel: A lot of guys that played with my dad back in the day, they say I skate a lot like my dad. He's kind of the same player as I am. I credit my speed to him but at the same time I've worked really hard on it. It's hard work in the summer. I think my dad has really helped me on my skating growing up. It's the biggest thing I've always had to work on. I think it's really benefitting me now. You know you've got to stick to your strengths. That's what I'm trying to do.

HP: You say you have to stick to your strengths but I'm sure someone would like to know what you say is your weakness that you have to fix?

Daniel: This year, so far, I think it's frustration, with the slump and everything before. I was kind of frustrated. Another thing could be that sometimes I over handle the puck and I shouldn't. I should wait or make it simple

.

HP: To close this off, like you mentioned at the very beginning, unfortunately for you, for two straight years now, the Sue St. Marie Greyhounds will not be in the playoffs. You have a lot of time to improve yourself behind closed doors before you get to the NHL draft combine where you get to show off your skills to improve that final ranking. I don't want to ask if you have a specific plan in mind but I'm sure you know what you're going to be working on to make yourself better, would that be correct?

Daniel: Hopefully I'll get an invite to the Team Canada under 18. I'll just go from there. If I make that tournament, when I get back, I'll go back to my gym with Gary Roberts and train up for the combine.

HP: First overall draft pick in 2009, you're a gold medal winner with Team Canada at the Ivan Helenka last year, you're a top prospect. Best of luck to you.

Daniel: Thank you.

Andrew Shaw
Center – Owen Sound Attack
Conducted May 9, 2011

My first memory of Andrew Shaw was back before he became a member of the Niagara Ice Dogs. I was helping out at the Dogs main camp and I was coaching one of the 6 teams that were put together for camp. Andrew was not on my team but I noticed him pretty quickly. Shaw showed exactly what you see from him today. He was a pest. He made himself one of the hardest workers on the ice. He crashed the net very hard and was a handful for opposing defensemen trying to handle him. When the round robin games were completed, Andrew Shaw, a player who was not supposed to make the team that fall had earned himself a roster spot. He kept rolling along. He scored in pre-season and set the tone for his rookie season in the OHL.

The next memory that stands out for me in his rookie season was a fight with Adrian Robertson of the Peterborough Petes. It was Shaw's first OHL fight and he pretty much destroyed the much bigger Robertson, and when the fight was over he got the Niagara fans cheering even louder when he mocked flashing a championship belt around his waist. That was the one of many examples in that rookie season that Shaw was tough and would do whatever he could to help his team win. Andrew showed as that season moved along that he was not afraid of any player in the league.

What many didn't see that rookie season, or the season that followed, was the other talents Shaw possessed. This was a player who had posted huge scoring numbers just months previous in Midget AAA. I watched Shaw in practice and saw a very underrated player that was clearly capable of playing in a top 6 in the OHL. Shaw understood the game and if you have ever watched one of his games in earshot of his parents (as I recently did) you would know exactly why. Both of Andrew's parents are intense and are very knowledgeable about the game. It's not hard to see that the apple didn't fall far from the tree. Andrew Shaw reminds me of "The Rat" Ken Linseman. He plays the same style. He can play on both the powerplay and the penalty kill. He can show toughness on one shift and show off a beautiful backhand to the top corner on his next shift.

I always felt if Shaw could get a bit more ice he would be able to show off what he was capable of doing in the OHL. A trade to start this season made Shaw a member of the Owen Sound Attack.

He was going to a team that wanted him, and to a team that thought he had more in him. Shaw posted just under a point per game including 22 goals. As I write this, he has chipped in another 19 points in 19 playoff games including 10 goals. I have watched 15 of Owen Sound's playoff games, including 10 live. Shaw has been one of the best players on the ice in most of the games.

I spoke to Shaw between games #4 and #5 of the OHL finals:

HP: Take me back to that rookie season. Tell me about your thought process leading up to the main camp in Niagara.

AS: I had looked at the roster before I arrived at camp and knew that they had lost a lot of forwards so I thought I could make the team. I just played as hard as I could and before the Black & White game Dave Brown (Niagara GM at the time) came up to me and said that they wanted to sign me.

HP: So you go on from there and obviously in your first season, I'm sure you were just happy to have made the team. When year two arrived did you have the thought process of it being your year to show what you could do? Take me through a bit of that season and who you played with etc...

AS: I ended year one with a good playoffs so I was hoping I would make the top six forwards. Mario Cicchillo really liked me but then he was fired. I wasn't sure what Mike McCourt thought of me. When I got to camp I was playing 3rd line Center with Hasson (Mike) and Johnson Andrews and then about 10 games in I was moved to the wing with Freddie Hamilton and Andrew Agozzino. I had 10 points in 10 games with them. Then coach came up to me and said that he was moving back to 3rd line. I pretty much played 3rd line the rest of the year with Andrews and Dylan MacEachern or Josh Moes. I did get some powerplay but we didn't get much time on the ice. Then playoffs came around and I was hurt so I didn't play much in playoffs at all.

HP: Ok, so year two comes to an end and obviously it was a bit of a rebuilding year for Niagara. Summertime comes and goes and next thing, you find yourself traded to a new city, Owen Sound. Take me through the first few weeks with Owen Sound and your first impressions.

AS: When I first got traded there, Dale (DeGray) and Mark (Reeds) both really seemed like they wanted me on their team which was exciting for me. They started telling me all the opportunity I was going to get. Once I got there, they had quite a few guys out of the lineup. They had guys still away at camp and Hish (Joey Hishon) was hurt there for a bit. I was pulling first line and first powerplay ice. When the guys came back they put me back on the 3rd line with Halmo and Childerly and our line was putting up just as many points as the 2nd line. I wasn't worried about my icetime because he (Mark Reeds) just rolled three lines. Our team started getting some publicity about how good we were - we went on that nine game win streak. I was really happy. I didn't mind playing 3rd line at all...it was my kind of role, you know, – I just wanted to bring a lot of energy. We got pucks deep and cycled in the corners – took pucks to the net. Playing with Halmo was good. He has a similar style as me so it worked out well with me and him. We played with each other all year and look what happened, we put up some pretty decent points and had some time on second powerplay. I think I had 7 or 9 powerplay goals.

HP: Obviously a strong season in Owen Sound for the whole team, not just yourself. Now you find yourself where every player would like to be (in the OHL Finals) and you're having an outstanding playoffs for yourself. I always thought you had offensive capabilities and I know you play ball hockey as well. Can you tell us about the award you won in ball hockey this year and speak about ball hockey as a summer activity leading up to a fall OHL season?

AS: In the summer I was over in Europe for Team Canada Ball hockey and Garrett Wilson was on my team as well. We ended up winning the gold with a 5-0 win in the finals. I got an award as MVP and Top Scorer and I made the All Star line. I like it because it keeps you in shape. We only had two lines and the games are an hour long. You are always running because there is no chance to glide like on the ice. Then I think it was about October I found out I got this award for International Player of the Year for Ball Hockey, which was pretty exciting. I had a bunch of people call me to congratulate me but I was more focused on ice hockey at the time so I haven't really had a chance to enjoy it yet. I want to focus on ice hockey right now and then I'll get a chance to enjoy the award after the season.

HP: I would imagine you arrive at OHL camp in good shape and that the ball hockey helps your hands as well.

AS: Yeah, like I said, we only have two lines so you are running all the time. I work out in the gym during the day and then play ball hockey at night. It's a good workout. My hands are not awesome or anything but everything I do have hands wise, is helped by ball hockey.

HP: Let's talk about you as a player. I'll pick a subject and you give me your thoughts. Let's start with skating. What do you think of your skating?

AS: I think I'm a pretty strong skater. I think I'm pretty fast out there. I think I'm quick starting and stopping in the corners. I find I'm kind of hard to knock off the puck, when guys put their weight into me I just lean back and they actually help me to go faster.

HP: So obviously 1 on 1 battles are a strength, your forecheck is a strength. Tell me about your thoughts of your defensive play.

AS: I think my defensive play has improved. I have gotten better every year but there is always room for improvement. Terry Virtue helped a lot this year with our D zone coverage. I think my play is better this year then it's been in past years and I hope it just gets better as I get older. I think I'm more instinctive now. I don't really think about where to go or what I need to do – I just naturally know what my job is and where I need to be. You learn a lot after three years in the league and Mark (Reeds) is always about where you need to be and holding your ice.

HP: Has he (Mark Reeds) changed his systems much this year, or has he pretty much driven home one main forecheck and one main defensive zone system?

AS: Our forecheck is usually always the same but depending on who we are playing against on the weekend ahead, he will change our neutral zone forecheck or our defensive zone coverage-just depending on how they play their game. This really helps out a lot because we know what they are going to do, and it makes it a little bit easier.

HP: I noticed against Windsor (playoffs) one of your neutral zones is sending two guys forcing their defensemen, and your own weak side defensemen played up on their winger. Then he (Reeds) seemed to switch it in mid game.

AS: Yeah, that was because of what Ellis (Ryan) was doing. He is pretty good at neutral zone transition for them – he will just drag the puck back and he will find a guy far side or something so we had to change it up.

HP: Let's talk about your shot. Tell me about your shot.

AS: This year it's much better. I had that broken wrist and it took a long time to recover that summer. So when I went into camp I couldn't shoot very much, I didn't have a hard shot like I did in my first year but I worked on it a lot. I did a lot of strengthening in my wrist where the injury happened and now I think it's better than ever. Clearly it shows this year that if you have a better shot, pucks go in I guess (laughs).

HP: You are on the ice, so you don't get a chance to hear them, but I recently was within earshot of your mother and father for a whole game. They are quite the pair as far as fans go. Have you had many people comment to you about them?

AS: (Laughs) Yeah they always say my dad is a great funny guy, umm...he is outgoing, he is always talking to everyone. They just say he is really friendly and he's funny. They say my mom is just like him, she is outgoing and you know playing hockey all my life my parents have got to know all the other parents and become friends with them. If they are at a game, they just have fun. They are really enjoying the winning this year. They come up to every home game (from Belleville) to watch every game. I think other fans really like them...they always come up to me and say that they met my dad and he's a great guy and moms' nice too...all that kind of stuff.

HP: So as I referred to, at a recent game in Owen Sound, I had them both within earshot. I can see where you get your style of play from and where you get your hockey smarts. Both your parents clearly know the game. I could hear your mom yelling out and almost coaching along on who was on the wrong side of the puck, etc. Have you had many comments made to you about their hockey knowledge?

AS: Oh yeah, well my mom gets so excited at games, she is always talking. She went to my dad's hockey games when she was 18 and she has been to games 3 times a week since then so she has learned the game very well and she loves it just as much as we do. Both my parents know what they are talking about, they know their stuff. That's why I always listened to my dad. He coached me when I was younger and was always there for me. He was always harder on me and that would make me better, it's paid off in the end.

HP: So you are in the OHL finals and like any player you must think about signing a pro contract. Have you spoken to any NHL teams or has Dale (DeGray) given you any feedback?

AS: My agent and Dale have both said good things but I have told them that I don't want to hear any of it until after the OHL Finals and the Memorial Cup. But I have heard good things, they just say keep playing hard. One of my teammates came up to me and said that his NHL team was watching me and asked about me. They really liked how I was playing and said to just keep doing what I have been doing. They loved the way I have been playing. So for the most part I just keep hearing to keep doing what I'm doing and good things will happen.

HP: Well Andrew, you have always worked hard. I wish you all the success you seek going forward and good luck the rest of the way in the OHL Finals and in the Memorial Cup.

AS: Thanks Mark.

Note: I wanted to include this short blurb and interview about Andrew Shaw because I feel strongly about him as a 1991 born player who has been passed over. HockeyProspect.com was founded based on a player that was 'under the radar' (Wayne Simmonds) and I think that Andrew has also flown low on radar. I don't know Andrew very well. I have had a few short conversations with him since he entered the league. This year I have seen him a few times after games and just had a few quick words with him. He has proven to be well spoken and polite in our conversations. I know his teammate Cameron Brace pretty well. Cameron speaks highly of Andrew.

Mark Edwards

Philippe Danault
Center – Victoriaville Tigres
Conducted February, 2011

HP: You are the captain of Victoriaville, and not only are you the youngest captain in the QMJHL, but also at the CHL, do you see that as an honor for yourself?

PD: Oh yes, for sure it's a very big honor for me and I will take this in my package to have a lot of experience. I have a lot of good players that are 20 years old that support me a lot. I'm captain but they help me a lot.

HP: Now you are a Victoriaville kid, so many people have seen you throughout the years rise through the ranks, so to speak. I am told that they expected you to be captain of the Tigres. Do you think that you're ready for that responsibility?

PD: Yes, for sure because I had a very good captain before me. He showed me the way and I just continued the same way. Everything is going good up to now because I am trying to do things the same way. I try to do my best every game and every shift. I don't change my game but it's just an honor and I take it in a good way.

HP: People say that you don't really grow into a leader, you are one. I expect since you have the "C" on your chest, you are that type of person, you are that strong leader. But you do learn from other guys, like you said, from Devos the previous captain for Victoriaville. What did you learn specifically from him, that'll help you be a better captain?

PD: When we lost he could slow down the game. It made it easier. He scored a lot of goals, he was a good shooter and stuff like that. He calmed down the team, he would tell us not to panic and make simple plays.

HP: You've had a phenomenal year thus far, not only personally, but with the CHL as well. You were in the Super Series, as well as the Top Prospects Game. I noticed that during the practice at the Top Prospects Game, I heard a lot of people talking about watching you and being very interested in what you could do. Specifically, with the Top Prospects Game. Did you find yourself in awe of where you were, like Toronto Air Canada Centre, and the amount of media that was there, was it a little overwhelming for you?

PD: No not at all. It was a good experience. For me just the experience...I dreamed of that, dream after dream. It's just an honor for me to be there. I don't have more stress with people talking about me because I have the "C" I just play my game and I will know what is going to happen after the season.

HP: You're one of the first, if not the first player, on the ice and one of the last off of it. Now I hear you're the same way when you practice with Victoriaville. Is that just the dedication that you have to practice, and learning and growing as a player, because you have the "C" on your chest, or is it because you've always had this discipline about you to give it all you have?

PD: No. seriously for me it's patience, is that the word? I just like to be on the ice and shoot the puck....just a desire to learn so I love it. For me it's not discipline or something like that. It's my passion. It's what I want to do for my life so that's why I'm always on the ice.

HP: Did you ever believe that you could be where you are right now, in such a very good draft position for the NHL Entry Draft?

PD: (Laughs) No, for sure not. I didn't believe it from when I was young. Again, it's a good experience. I don't have any words to describe this moment in my life...the last two years, it's been so amazing for me and I'm never going to forget it.

HP: As I said, a lot of people were talking about you, what you bring to the game, each and every night, and the quick scouting report on you is that you were a very fast skater. You can skate very well, you provide a lot of offensive skill for your wingers because you are a center-man. But you are also small, and that you "lack the finish" that some people might want from a centerman. With this being said about you, what do you believe is your game, how accurate would you say that scouting report is?

PD: I think the scouting report is that I'm a good player that can bring energy and can play both ends of the ice. I have leadership, so that why they like me too. Also my energy and my intensity and my desire to win too...so if you have the desire to win, you have good things that are going to happen.

HP: Now are you happy with your current play and your statistics at the moment, or would you maybe have expected that you would be doing a little better than you currently are?

160

PD: No. I'm very happy with my play on the ice now but I always want more and more and more. That is why I'm going to get better, that's why I practice every day to be better. I just work and the good things will happen.

HP: You've always had a connection to Victoriaville, you grew up in the town, and you're father was the PA announcer for the team, so not only are you connected because you live in the town, but because the connection that your family has through the Tigres. Having that closeness that closeness through the team, through your father, does it make it that much more special for you to play for the Tigres, at least this far in your Q career?

PD: Yes, for sure. It's an experience I have lived my whole life. I was so young, every game I would go see the Tigres players after the game, and now it's me. I'm the Tigres. It's a good feeling for me. I know what the young kids want. I was the same as them so its' just amazing for me.

HP: And with that said, you watched a lot of Tigre games, is there a former player that maybe you modeled your game after a little bit?

PD: Yes, for sure. I learned about this game and it's why I'm there now. I just learned off that and my father. I got to watch every game free (laughs) – I learned off players for sure but I learned from my practice and my coaches. It's why I'm here now.

HP: One thing that is always stressed, not just in the QMJHL, but throughout the entire CHL, is giving back and supporting the community that pays money to watch you young men play. You being a local kid, I presume it is of high importance that you give back to the community that supports not only yourself, but the team?

PD: Yes, for sure. We play to have fun and the people come to see us and we win to so it's beautiful to see players playing hard and all the players play hard in both ends of the ice. It's a show, but at the same time we work hard and it's like our job.

HP: Phillip, one more question for you: to take your game to that next level, to improve not only yourself, but your draft ranking, what do you believe that you have to accomplish by the end of the season to take yourself to that next step?

PD: I want to be more physical with my upper body. I want to be stronger with my legs and my upper body. I want to have a better wrist shot. That is what I want to improve from now until the end of the season.

*** Phillip did this interview with us in English. It should be noted that English is his second language. We appreciate him making the time for us.*

Mark Scheifele
Center – Barrie Colts
Conducted November 2010

HP: Certainly the start to your season and your career in the Ontario Hockey League has been a good one. What has been the biggest transition coming from Junior B to Junior A?

MS: Definitely just the speed, the pace of the game. You don't have as much time with the puck, and you really have to think quick. Also, the strength of the players, because everyone's strong, everyone can play the game well. You just really have to be strong every night and be consistent.

HP: Now you had a four-year scholarship opportunity to Cornell University and you chose to come to the Barrie Colts after your rights were traded from Saginaw. What made you decide to go that route?

MS: Really just going over the pros and cons of the NCAA and OHL and really seeing how good of a program Barrie does have. Being that this is my draft year and really being one of my biggest years, I was just thinking that this is a really good shot for me. I thought I'd get lots of playing time and make an impact.

HP: Not only that, but you have a Hall-of-Fame NHL player as your coach that's just come into Barrie in Dale Hawerchuk. How have you found him as a coach and mentor for you?

MS: He's been unreal. He's really taught me a lot with faceoffs, my shot, my hands. Just a sense of the game, he really knows exactly what you need to do to succeed and knows exactly how to teach you.

HP: You're a forward now, but I understand you played defense all the way up through AAA. What made you change to a forward from that point on?
MS: My one coach just put me at forward and told me I'd be there for a couple games. I did really well, and he kept me there for the entire year. I just kind of picked it up quickly and started to really enjoy it.

HP: You're among the OHL rookie scoring leaders. Did you have a goal in mind when you entered the season as to what you might want to accomplish this year?

MS: Really just to play my game. I know if I play my game, points will come. So, really just to play my hardest. My goal is to get a point a game, but my main goal is to help my team succeed.

HP: Now on the academic side, I noticed that you were selected as the Academic Player of the Month for October for the Central Division. Obviously, schooling must be a very big focus for you?

MS: It is. I've always strived to get high marks in school. I find it helps that if you're smart in class, you'll be smart on the ice. My parents have always brought me up to work hard in school, and they've always been on me about my grades. I don't find it too difficult to hold your marks if you're doing your homework and studying.

HP: Is there something in particular that you're focusing on to refine in your game?

MS: Just little things like working on my draws, stopping and starting. I'm really just working on things that help our team succeed. I've been working on defensive play, because I know that defense does create offense when you create turnovers.

HP: Is there somebody in particular in the NHL that you might model your game after or compare yourself to?

MS: Well, I've always liked watching Steve Yzerman. He's been my favorite player forever. I really like his work ethic, defensive play and his offense. Now that he's retired, my favorite player is Pavel Datsyuk. I try to model my game a bit around him, just how he's an overall good player. He's won the Frank Selke award a bunch of years for being the best defensive forward, so I try to incorporate that part of his game into mine. I also watch Youtube videos of him all the time doing little dangles and stuff, but I picture myself as more of a Jason Spezza on the offensive end.

HP: Is the CHL Top Prospects Game some sort of goal that you want to earn your way into that game?
MS: Yeah, definitely. I set goals every month and that was definitely one of my high-end goals.

HP: You were raised in Kitchener, Ontario and that's your hometown. Of course you were playing Junior B there last year. Does that make you a Kitchener Rangers fan growing up now converted to Barrie?

MS: I've been to many of their games growing up and always liked to watch them play. But I play for Barrie, so they're definitely my No. 1 team. But when we played Kitchener in October, it was cool to be able to play in that building and play against a team that I grew up watching.

HP: When you look at the Barrie Colts, I guess you could call them in rebuilding mode after they went after an OHL championship last year, but can you give us a sizing up of the talent that you might see on that club?

MS: We do have a lot of young players that are starting to adapt. Like Zach Hall, who actually had a broken wrist, he's a really solid player. We have some solid skating defensemen. Clint Windsor, who's a very good goalie, is someone I can see being a top goalie in years to come. Some of our older guys will also help us in our rebuilding year.

HP: Jeff Skinner, a former Ranger, is leading rookies in scoring with about a point a game so far. Does that give you hope that you could get there sooner rather than later?

MS: Yeah, definitely. Youth is a huge part of the NHL now. It's all about being quick. It's all about having the agility and the skill to be able to play in that league. Definitely seeing Jeff play in Kitchener and seeing him adapt to the NHL, you just see how much improvement you can go through just by playing with those guys. It's definitely nice to see that some of these guys can stick so early in their careers.

Brett Ritchie
Right Wing – Sarnia Sting
Conducted May 9, 2011

HP: Going from being a rookie, to an NHL Draft Eligible sophomore in the OHL, what kind of adjustments did you have to make from the two seasons?

BR: A lot of adjustments were made throughout my first two seasons in the OHL. Initially as a rookie you get used to the speed and size of the competition, but once you become acclimatized to that, you start looking for ways to outplay the opposing players and get the upper hand. This only comes with experience and its something your striving for throughout each season.

HP: You had an infection in your Elbow, mono, then suffered an injury to your knee over the course of this season. How did this affect your mentality throughout the season, and what did you do to maintain focus?

BR: I was very unfortunate with some fluke injuries this season especially with the mono half way through the season. It was extremely tough mentally, especially in the midst of such an important year. I tried to focus on doing whatever I could to recover as quicky as possible knowing there is no way of controlling how it happened. In each illness or injury I had this season I came back sooner than expected which was a bonus.

HP: We saw you go down awkwardly in your last shift at the World Under 18 Championships? How are you doing now, and are there any lingering effects from this?

BR: I hit my bare hip along the ledge of the boards, it pinched a nerve on my hip flexor and seized up my leg for an hour or so. It was extremely painful but the pain subsided with a few hours after and all I was left with was a bone bruise on the front of my hip.

HP: Despite playing for a young Sarnia team, what positive influences did you receive from veteran players?

BR: We have some great leadership on our team in Sarnia. Starting with our captain Nathan Chiarlitti. He is great with working with young kids and new players in the league and has a professional attitude on and off the ice. Other examples of solid veteran presence on our team is Joe Rogalski, Daniel Broussard, and graduated player Kale Kerbashian.

HP: Please describe yourself as a player, and highlight your strengths, and the area(s) in which you would like to improve?

BR: I think i play a typical power forward game. I use my size and reach to my advantage to win puck battles and play physical. I also think I have a good shot and provide a good net presence.

HP: Have you been following where different services are ranking you, and does it stick in the back of your mind at all?

BR: I try not to pay attention to that stuff. I would say the only one I know is the NHL Central Scouting rankings. I don't think these rankings affect me or my game at all.

HP: You played internationally for Canada twice this year, can you tell us what that was like for you, and how you feel you did at those tournaments?

BR: Playing for your country is one of the best experiences you can accomplish. Wearing the maple leaf is an unbelievable feeling that you're not going find anywhere else. I thought I played well in both of those tournaments especially in the summer where we won gold.

HP: Who are your favorite NHL Players? Do they influence your game at all or do you pattern your game after any NHLers?

BR: My favorite NHL player is Ryan Getzlaf. I watch him and try and pick up things he does and for sure, I try to model my game around his. Other guys who I think i may resemble are Corey Perry, David Backes or Ryan Clowe.

HP: What is your favorite pre-game meal? Have you focused yet on your diet and in-taking the proper foods, or is that something you still intend to work on?

BR: My favorite pre-game meal is breaded chicken breasts, with penne pasta and a blush sauce. diet is important to me. Although I'm not a health nut, I do watch what I eat.

HP: Training wise, can you take us through a typical day of working out for Brett Ritchie?

BR: That a hard question to answer, because each day we tend to focus on something different whether it's cardio, footwork, power lifting or upper/lower body training. But regardless I try to incorporate a bit of everything into every workout.

HP: How much does your training schedule differ from the Winter months to the Summer.

BR: In the winter in Sarnia we usually train light 2-4 times a week doing low weight and high reps with a a lot of plyometric work and biking. In the summer it is much more intense going 5 days a week doing vigorous cardio and lifting each workout.

HP: Over the course of this season, who was the toughest player to play/battle against along the boards, and in the corners?

BR: A guy like Zack Kassian is probably one of the toughest to battle with. He is so big and strong that most guys have a real tough time pushing him around or taking the puck from him.

HP: Who were the toughest defensemen to beat 1 on 1 that you faced throughout the season.

BR: I would have to say Brett Flemming from Mississauga. He is very underrated I think. He plays a great gap and has great feet, which makes him tough to beat.

HP Thanks again for your time Brett, We appreciate it.

BR: Thank you.

3

TEAM REPORTS

ATLANTA THRASHERS

Top Five:

1) Paul Postma, Defense, AHL
2) Carl Klingberg, Forward, AHL
3) Spencer Machacek, Forward, AHL
4) Julian Melchiori, Defense, OHL
5) Ivan Telegin, Forward, OHL

2011 Potential Draft Targets (7th Overall Pick)

1) Ryan Strome
2) Ryan Murphy
3) Nathan Beaulieu

ANAHEIM DUCKS

Top Five:

1) Emerson Etem, Forward, WHL
2) Peter Holland, Forward, OHL
3) Justin Schultz, Defense, NCAA
4) Kyle Palmieri, Forward, AHL
5) Devante Smith-Pelly, Forward, OHL

2011 Potential Draft Targets (22nd Overall Pick)

1) Tyler Biggs
2) Brett Ritchie
3) Vladislav Namestnikov

BOSTON BRUINS

Top Five:

1) Jared Knight, Forward, OHL
2) Ryan Spooner, Forward, OHL
3) Jordan Caron, Forward, AHL
4) Matt Bartkowski, Defense, AHL
5) Maxime Sauve, Forward, AHL

2011 Potential Draft Targets (9th Overall Pick - Toronto)

1) Ryan Murphy
2) Ryan Strome
3) Mika Zibanejad

BUFFALO SABRES

Top Five:

1) Zack Kassian, Forward, OHL
2) T.J Brennan, Defense, AHL
3) Luke Adam, Forward, AHL
4) Jhonas Enroth, Goalie, AHL
5) Marcus Foligno, Forward, OHL

2011 Potential Draft Targets (16th Overall Pick)

1) Tyler Biggs
2) Scott Mayfield
3) Jonas Brodin

CAROLINA HURRICANES

Top Five:

1) Justin Faulk, Defense, NCAA
2) Zach Boychuk, Forward, AHL
3) Zac Dalpe, Forward, AHL
4) Brian Dumoulin, Defense, NCAA
5) Riley Nash, Forward, AHL

2011 Potential Draft Targets (12th Overall Pick)

1) Joel Armia
2) Sven Bartschi
3) Jamie Oleksiak

CALGARY FLAMES

Top Five:

1) Tim Erixon, Defense, SEL
2) Max Reinhart, Forward, WHL
3) Greg Nemisz, Forward, AHL
4) T.J Brodie, Defense, AHL
5) Ryan Howse, Forward, WHL

2011 Potential Draft Targets (13th Overall Pick)

1) Jamieson Oleskiak
2) Mark McNeill
3) Duncan Siemens

CHICAGO BLACKHWKS

Top Five:

1) Jeremy Morin, Forward, AHL/NHL
2) Dylan Olsen, Defense, NCAA/AHL
3) Jimmy Hayes, Forward, NCAA
4) Kyle Beach, Forward, AHL
5) Kevin Hayes, Forward, NCAA

2011 Potential Draft Targets (18th Overall Pick)

1) Oscar Klefbom
2) Jamieson Oleskiak
3) Scott Mayfield

COLORADO AVALANCHE

Top Five:

1) Tyson Barrie, Defense,
2) Joey Hishon, Forward,
3) Stefan Elliott, Defense, WHL
4) Calvin Pickard, Goalie, WHL
5) Cameron Gaunce, Defense, AHL

2011 Potential Draft Targets (2nd and 11th -St. Louis)

1) Gabriel Landeskog
2) Adam Larsson
3) Jonathan Huberdeau
4) Duncan Siemens
5) Ty Rattie
6) Mark McNeill

COLUMBUS BLUE JACKETS

Top Five:

1) Ryan Johansen, Forward, WHL
2) John Moore, Defense, AHL/NHL
3) David Savard, Defense, AHL
4) Cody Goloubef, Defense, AHL
5) Cam Atkinson, Forward, NCAA

2011 Potential Draft Targets (8th Overall Pick)

1) Nathan Beaulieu
2) Ryan Murphy
3) Ryan Strome

DALLAS STARS

Top Five:

1) Jack Campbell, Goalie, OHL
2) Scott Glennie, Forward, WHL
3) Alex Chiasson, Forward, NCAA
4) Philip Larsen, Defense, AHL/NHL
5) Reilly Smith, Forward, NCAA

2011 Potential Draft Targets (14th Overall Pick)

1) Jamieson Oleskiak
2) Duncan Siemens
3) Ryan Sproul

DETROIT RED WINGS

Top Five:

1) Brendan Smith, Defense, AHL
2) Tomas Tatar, Forward, AHL
3) Gustav Nyquist, Forward, NCAA
4) Teemu Pulkinnen, Forward, SM-Liiga
5) Riley Sheahan, Forward, NCAA

2011 Potential Draft Targets (24th Overall)

1) Tomas Jurco
2) Mark Scheifele
3) Stuart Percy

EDMONTON OILERS

Top Five:

1) Tyler Pitlick, Forward, WHL
2) Martin Marincin, Defense, WHL
3) Curtis Hamilton, Forward, WHL
4) Ryan Martindale, Forward, OHL
5) Olivier Roy, Goalie, QMJHL

2011 Potential Draft Targets (1st Overall) (19th Los Angeles)

1) Ryan Nugent-Hopkins   1) Jonas Brodin
2) Adam Larsson   2) Duncan Siemens
3) Gabriel Landeskog   3) Joe Morrow

FLORIDA PANTHERS

Top Five:

1) Jacob Markstrom, Goalie, AHL
2) Erik Gudbranson, Defense, OHL
3) Nick Bjugstad, Forward, NCAA
4) Quinton Howden, Forward, WHL
5) Alexander Petrovic, Defense, WHL

2011 Potential Draft Targets (3rd Overall)

1) Adam Larsson
2) Gabriel Landeskog
3) Ryan Nugent-Hopkins

LOS ANGELES KINGS

Top Five:

1) Brayden Schenn, Forward, NHL/WHL
2) Tyler Toffoli, Forward, OHL
3) Derek Forbort, Defense, NCAA
4) Vyacheslav Voynov, Defense, AHL
5) Thomas Hickey, Defense, AHL

2011 Potential Draft Targets (No 1st Round Pick)

1) _____
2) _____
3) _____

MINNESOTA WILD

Top Five:

1) Mikael Granlund, Forward, SM- Liiga
2) Jason Zucker, Forward, NCAA
3) Erik Haula, Forward, NCAA
4) Matt Hackett, Goaltender, AHL
5) Brett Bulmer, Forward, WHL

2011 Potential Draft Targets (10th Overall Pick)

1) Ryan Strome
2) Ryan Murphy
3) Boone Jenner

MONTREAL CANADIENS

Top Five:

1) Danny Kristo, Forward, NCAA
2) Jarred Tinordi, Defense, OHL
3) Louis Leblanc, Forward, QMJHL
4) Aaron Palushaj, Forward, AHL
5) Michael Bournival, Forward, QMJHL

2011 Potential Draft Targets (17th Overall Pick)

1) Oscar Klefbom
2) Boone Jenner
3) Joel Armia

NASHVILLE PREDATORS

Top Five:

1) Jonathon Blum, Defense, AHL/NHL
2) Ryan Ellis, Defense, OHL
3) Taylor Beck, Forward, OHL
4) Roman Josi, Defense, AHL
5) Austin Watson, Forward, OHL

2011 Potential Draft Targets (No 1st Round Pick)

1) _____
2) _____
3) _____

NEW JERSEY DEVILS

Top Five:

1) Jon Merrill, Defense, NCAA
2) Adam Henrique, Forward, AHL
3) Alexander Urbom, Defense, AHL
4) Eric Gelinas, Defense, QMJHL
5) Brandon Burlon, Defense, NCAA

2011 Potential Draft Targets (4th Overall)

1) Ryan Strome
2) Jonathan Huberdeau
3) Gabriel Landeskog

NEW YORK ISLANDERS

Top Five:

1) Nino Niederriter, Forward, WHL/NHL
2) Calvin de Haan, Defense, OHL
3) Matt Donovan, Defense, NCAA
4) Anders Lee, Forwrad, NCAA
5) Brock Nelson, Forward, NCAA

2011 Potential Draft Targets (5th Overall)

1) Sean Couturier
2) Mika Zibanejad
3) Ryan Murphy

NEW YORK RANGERS

Top Five:

1) Chris Kreider, Forward, NCAA
2) Christian Thomas, Forward, OHL
3) Dylan McIlrath, Defense, WHL
4) Carl Hagelin, Forward, NCAA
5) Ryan Bourque, Forward, QMJHL

2011 Potential Draft Targets (15th Overall Pick)

1) Duncan Siemens
2) Mark McNeill
3) Joe Morrow

OTTAWA SENATORS

Top Five:

1) Jared Cowen, Defense, WHL
2) David Rundblad, Defense, SEL
3) Robin Lehner, Goalie, AHL
4) Louie Caporusso, Forward, NCAA
5) Patrick Wiercioch, Defense, AHL

2011 Potential Draft Targets (6th Overall) (21st Nashville)

1) Sean Couturier	1) Tyler Biggs
2) Ryan Murphy	2) Jonas Brodin
3) Dougie Hamilton	3) Oscar Klefbom

PHILADELPHIA FLYERS

Top Five:

1) Erik Gustafsson, Defense, AHL
2) Erik Wellwood, Forward, AHL
3) Brendan Ranford Forward, WHL
4) Jason Akeson, Forward, OHL
5) Mark Testwuide, Forward, AHL

2011 Potential Draft Targets (No 1st Round Pick):

1) _____
2) _____
3) _____

PHOENIX COYOTES

Top Five:

1) Brandon Gormley, Defense, QMJHL
2) Brett MacLean, Forward, AHL
3) Maxim Goncharov, Defense, AHL
4) Mark Visentin, Goalie, OHL
5) Phil Lane, Forward, OHL

2011 Potential Draft Targets (20th Overall Pick)

1) Rocco Grimaldi
2) Nicklas Jensen
3) Joseph Morrow

PITTSBURGH PENGUINS

Top Five:

1) Simon Despres, Defense, QMJHL
2) Tom Kuhnhackl, Forward, OHL
3) Beau Bennett, Forward, NCAA
4) Brad Thiessen, Goalie, AHL
5) Ken Agostino, Forward, NCAA

2011 Potential Draft Targets (23rd Overall Pick)

1) Tyler Biggs
2) Tomas Jurco
3) Stuart Percy

SAN JOSE SHARKS

Top Five:

1) Charlie Coyle, Forward, NCAA
2) Alex Stalock, Goalie, AHL
3) Taylor Doherty, Defense, OHL
4) Nick Petrecki, Defense, AHL
5) Freddie Hamilton, Forward, OHL

2011 Potential Draft Targets (27-30 Range)

1) Nicklas Jensen
2) Shane Prince
3) Tomas Jurco

ST.LOUIS BLUES

Top Five:

1) Jaden Schwartz, Forward, NCAA
2) Vladimir Tarasenko, Forward, KHL
3) Jake Allen, Goalie, AHL
4) Mark Cundari, Defense, AHL
5) Jonas Junland, Defense, SEL

2011 Potential Draft Targets (No 1st Round Pick):

1) _____
2) _____
3) _____

TAMPA BAY LIGHTNING

Top Five:

1) Brett Connolly, Forward, WHL
2) Carter Ashton, Forward, WHL
3) Dustin Tokarski, Goalie, AHL
4) Richard Panik, Forward, OHL
5) Johan Harju, Forward, AHL

2011 Potential Draft Targets (27-30 Range)

1) Tyler Biggs
2) Scott Mayfield
3) Vladislav Namestnikov

TORONTO MAPLE LEAFS

Top Five:

1. Joe Colborne (Forward, AHL)
2. Jake Gardiner (Defense, NCAA/AHL)
3. Greg McKegg (Forward, OHL)
4. Matt Frattin (Forward, NCAA)
5. Jesse Blacker (Defense, OHL)

2011 Potential Draft Targets (25th Overall Pick) (27 -30 Range)

1. Stuart Percy
2. Matt Puempel
3. Tyler Biggs

VANCOUVER CANUCKS

Top Five:

1) Cody Hodgson, Forward, AHL
2) Jordan Schroeder, Forward, AHL
3) Sergei Shirokov, Forward, AHL
4) Anton Rodin, Forward, SEL
5) Billy Sweatt, Forward, AHL

2011 Potential Draft Targets (27-30 Range):

1) Tomas Jurco
2) Vladislav Namestnikov
3) Ryan Sproul

WASHINGTON CAPITALS

Top Five:

1) Evgeny Kuznetsov, Forward, KHL
2) Cody Eakin, Forward, WHL
3) Patrick Wey, Defense, NCAA
4) Stanislav Galiev, Forward, QMJHL
5) Samuel Carrier, Defense, QMJHL

2011 Potential Draft Targets (26th Overall Pick)

1) Brett Ritchie
2) Brandon Saad
3) Vladislav Namestnikov

4

2012
NHL Draft Prospects

Nail Yakupov

Right Wing – Sarnia Sting (OHL)
Born Oct 6 1993 - Nizhnekamsk, Russia
Height 5.10 - Weight 170 - Shoots L

HOCKEYPROSPECT.COM

DRAFT GUIDE' 11

Games	Goals	Assists	Points	PIMS	+/-
65	49	52	101	71	-2

Nail Yakupov absolutely flew onto the scene for the Sarnia Sting after being drafted 2nd overall in the 2010 CHL Import draft. Yakupov broke Steven Stamkos' franchise rookie records in both Goals and Points. Nail narrowly missed the 50 goal mark, and is expected to absolutely dominate the OHL next season.

Yakupov has explosive speed, but uses an awkward hunched over style when skating that takes a little getting used to, and makes him look smaller than he is, but regardless it works for him. Acceleration is just as strong, and he is extremely shifty and elusive.

Despite his great skating abilities, Yakupov's standout skill has to be his shot, primarily his one timers, HP scout Ryan Yessie elaborates: "I was at training camp for the Sting, and during Yakupov's first scrimmage, Yakupov unloaded a one-timer that stunned the few hundred in attendance. Few NHLers can unload a shot like his, and here's a 16 year old rookie unloading it. It was then, myself and everyone in attendance realized the hype surrounding Yakupov was very real."

One side of Nail that doesn't get as much exposure at times is his physical play. He once checked an opponent through the glass. In several games, he had the biggest hit of the game. Yakupov has scored some highlight reel goals for Sarnia, and took advantage of the Sting's poor season by tearing up the U18 tournament, which included a hat trick in the bronze medal game, forcing the Canadian team to return home without a medal for the second straight year.

It's hard to watch Yakupov and not compare him to Washington's Alexander Ovechkin; he has the devastating goal scoring ability, skating, and can throw some massive hits. Although a few inches shorter, this comparison should follow him into his draft year. The only thing we'd like to see improve in Yakupov's game is his attention to the defensive aspect. He doesn't need to become a defensive player, just ensure he is not a liability in his own zone.

Mikhail Grigorenko

Center – CSKA-Krasnaja (MHL)
Born May 16 1994 - Khabarovsk, RUS
Height 6.02 - Weight 183 - Shoots L

HOCKEYPROSPECT.COM

DRAFT GUIDE' 11

Games	Goals	Assists	Points	PIMS	+/-
38	13	17	30	22	NA

Grigorenko has been considered a top prospect for several years for the 2012 draft. Until recently he had not been touched by any other Russian prospect other than Sarnia's Nail Yakupov, in terms of potential. Yakupov may have even surpassed him; however, Grigorenko has a ton of ability and potential moving forward. His 6'2" 185 pound frame promotes all of his abilities, and is fairly impressive for a player his age to already have that kind of size.

Grigorenko plays on a championship MHL team in Russia's junior league captained by Nikita Kucherov, who is one of the top Russians for the 2011 NHL Entry Draft. It was previously the home to the 2009 1st Overall selection in the 2009 KHL draft, and New York Rangers prospect defenseman Mikhail Pashnin.

Grigorenko has shown an outstanding amount of offensive potential. He enters the offensive zone with confidence and seems to know where he needs to be. He loves to have the puck on his stick; however, he proved at the U18's that he can also distribute the puck, leading the tournament in assists. Mikhail has strong puck control skills. He is very difficult to stop once he has possession because of his size and his great hands. Grigorenko has shown off some slick moves one on one and has shown off some highlight reel goals. His shot is hard and he has on occasion shown the willingness to use his body.

Grigorenko will likely see some time in the KHL. We expect him to be the top Russian player playing in Russia to get selected in the 2012 NHL Entry Draft. The big question is when will he make the jump over to North America, or will he remain in Russia for years. This question has affected the draft selection of a few Russian prospects in the past. Fellow U18 standout Nail Yakupov may be one Russian that does go extremely early. There is a very outside chance this sort of potential could convince Grigorenko to come to the CHL next year; however, we don't expect it.

Nick Ebert

Defense – Windsor Spitfires (OHL)
Born May 11 1994 -- Livingston, NJ
Height 6.01 -- Weight 195 -- Shoots R

DRAFT GUIDE' 11

Games	Goals	Assists	Points	PIMS	+/-
64	11	30	41	44	-2

Nick Ebert was drafted 17th Overall by the Mississauga St. Michael's Majors. Nick's stock fell in the OHL draft due to fears of Ebert not reporting. He was widely considered the best defenseman available in 2010. After being unable to come to terms with the St. Michael's Majors which would have secured a Memorial Cup trip in his rookie season, Ebert joined the defending champion Windsor Spitfires, and immediately reported to their team. Ebert put up great point totals, he was the highest scoring rookie defenseman, and landed in the top 15 of defenseman scoring league wide with an impressive class of defensemen in in front of him.

Ebert has great skating ability, can rush the puck up the ice with confidence and is extremely effective in doing so. He also is capable on the power play, moving the puck around, and has good vision. His point shot, when he used it, was effective; however, he appeared unwilling to use it very often.

Defensively Ebert is effective when in proper positioning; however, he occasionally appeared a little out of sorts on where he should be on the ice. However, it's to be expected of a 16 year old rookie. We would like to see him use his size more effectively. Ebert really doesn't have a big mean streak, but he is still young and this should develop next season. He has a lot of the size necessary to throw effective hits. It doesn't appear to be based on a lack of strength, compared to the average 16 year old OHL player.

A good workout schedule based on building upper body strength would be ideal for Ebert. He has the skating ability, and the offensive awareness and abilities to be a very high pick in 2012. He will be amongst the best defenseman eligible for next year's draft.

Alex Galchenyuk

Center – Sarnia Sting (OHL)
Born Feb 12, 1994 - Milwaukee, WI
Height 6.01 - Weight 185 - Shoots L

Games	Goals	Assists	Points	PIMS	+/-
68	31	52	83	52	-8

Alex Galchenyuk's journey was longer than most 1st Overall picks in the OHL Priority Selection. Born in Milwaukee, Alex played youth hockey in Italy, Russia, then eventually returning to the United States setting up shop in Chicago, before moving to Sarnia after being selected by the Sting. Alex was fairly well hidden throughout the year putting up stats that overwhelmed current NHLer's numbers when playing at that level. Galchenyuk was immediately put into a top six role with the Sting, and Galchenyuk didn't disappoint. Alex scored a goal in each of the first 5 games of his career. Galchenyuk would continue to put up points in a fairly consistent basis throughout the year, and finished 2nd in the OHL in rookie scoring.

Galchenyuk has outstanding hands, especially for a 16 year old, and has the ability to elude multiple opponents at once. Galchenyuk's bread and butter is his stickhandling, and overall control of the puck.

If Yakupov was the goal scorer, then Galchenyuk was the playmaker. Although he will try to do too much on his own at times, he has tremendous passing abilities, and can make high difficulty passes wherever he is on the ice. Galchenyuk is extremely difficult to defend. He has both options available to him. Alex's defensive game needs improvement, but he did spend time near the end of the season on the penalty kill, helping him improve on this aspect. We would also like him to use his size more effectively. He appears to be between 6'1" and 6'2" and he protects the puck well, but his play without the puck doesn't see enough physicality.

HP scout Ryan Yessie elaborates on Galchenyuk: "Alex is an extremely exciting player to watch. Very dynamic, and can create offense just as well as he can finish it. He can frustrate as at times he tries to do too much, he will stickhandle around two defenders, have an open shot, but instead choose to stickhandle around two more, and ends up losing his shooting angle. Alex possesses a great deal of potential, and I could see #1 AND #2 overall out of Sarnia in 2012."

Daniel Altshuller

Goalie – Nepean (CHL)
Born Jul 24, 1994 - Nepean, Ont.
Height 6.03 - Weight 195

HOCKEYPROSPECT.COM

DRAFT GUIDE' 11

Games	Wins	Losses	G.A.A	Save%	SO
43	19	13	3.22	.906	1

NHL teams love the big goalies, and Altshuller fits that bill. The Nepean, Ontario native still has his NCAA eligibility and probably will not sign with the Belleville Bulls until a goalie is moved. We expect the Bulls to trade Tyson Teichmann during the summer. Daniel moves well and will enter the 2011/2012 season as one of the highly touted goaltenders available for the 2012 NHL Draft. He had a strong showing in Winnipeg this past December posting great numbers for team Ontario including a .924 save percentage. Altshuller tracks the puck well and shows a high level of concentration, he seldom looks out of control. If he signs in Belleville he could compete with the very solid Malcom Subban right away - talk about a great goaltending tandem.

Brendan Gaunce

Center – Belleville Bulls (OHL)
Born Mar 25 1994 - Markham, ONT
Height 6.02 - Weight 205 - Shoots L

Games	Goals	Assists	Points	PIMS	+/-
65	11	25	36	40	-31

There was plenty of question as to where Brendan would go in the 2010 OHL Draft, but on draft day he didn't have to wait long. The Belleville Bulls made him the 2nd Overall pick, out the Markham Waxers program. Despite six total Waxers being selected in the 2010 OHL Draft, Brendan was the only one to appear in the OHL during the 2010-2011 season. Brendan is the younger brother of former Mississauga St. Michael's Majors defenseman Cameron Gaunce, who was known for his solid two-way ability and hockey sense. Brendan exhibits the same traits.

Gaunce came flying out of the gate as a rookie for the Bulls. In many of the games we watched he was one of the best Belleville players. Inconsistency can be expected out of a young developing forward. Brendan did have his ups and downs with mild slumps. When he's on, Gaunce will drive the net hard, and shows great confidence with the puck. Gaunce makes good decisions when entering the offensive zone between passing and driving the puck based on the situation around him. He already showed signs of owning the boards as youngster in the league. This is a sign of great things to come.

Gaunce has a good shot, and is very well positioned in the offensive zone. He keeps his stick on the ice, and does a lot of the little things right. Defensively, Gaunce may have learned from his brother, as he has shown very good knowledge of his responsibilities in the defensive zone. This proved to be very valuable at times for the young Bulls team. Brendan has also seen some time on the penalty kill for the Bulls.

With the move of at least two Bulls forwards from last year, the team could be wide open for a player like Brendan to walk into camp in September and take over permanent first line responsibilities. He is going to make Belleville a team to watch next year. We expect him to take a good run at becoming a 1st rounder in the 2012 NHL Entry Draft.

Mathew Campagna

Center – Sudbury Wolves (OHL)
Born Mar 9 1994 - Mississauga, ONT
Height 5.11 - Weight 170 - Shoots L

Games	Goals	Assists	Points	PIMS	+/-
58	7	17	24	36	-13

Going into the 2010 OHL Priority Selection, Mathew Campagna was considered one of the best, if not the best player in the draft. Mathew ended up slipping to 5th Overall where the Sudbury Wolves grabbed him up. Mathew came from a stacked program which also included fellow first rounders Luke Mercer and Jesse Graham, both of whom went to the Niagara Ice Dogs, and Cosimo Fontana who cracked the Ottawa 67s line-up.

The Wolves had decent depth going into this season at the forward position so Campagna switched between 2nd and 3rd line duties throughout the season.

Mathew handles the puck very well, with quick hands and elusive stickhandling. He also has the capability to score some highlight reel goals. Campagna is a solid skater, and has very good acceleration and quickness, and carries the puck with confidence. Unlike some smaller 16 year olds that enter the league, Mathew showed a willingness to take hits to make plays, and despite his size he appears committed to doing what it takes to help his team win. Campagna proved this toughness a few times. Despite not being quite 6ft. yet, he has dropped the gloves a number of times this season, and actually did pretty well for himself. Mathew is a disciplined player, only receiving 8 minor penalties all season.

The Wolves are expected to lose at least 3 of their top forwards from last year, which will open the door for a few players, one of them being Mathew. He will enter his draft year with key minutes for a team with good young potential.

Martin Frk

RW – Halifax (QMJHL)
Born Oct 5 1993 - Karlov ,Czech Rep.
Height 6.00 - Weight 198 - Shoots L

DRAFT GUIDE' 11

Games	Goals	Assists	Points	PIMS	+/-
62	22	28	50	75	-14

Martin Frk has been widely considered a Top 5 prospect for the 2012 NHL Entry Draft. The Halifax Mooseheads were able to talk Frk into reporting for the 2010-2011 season. Before joining the Mooseheads, Frk was a standout in the Karlovy Vary program known for developing some great Czech players. He put up well over a point per game in his two years with the U20 team. In the 2009-2010 season he also put up 186 penalty minutes; which is not something you expect to see out of a high end prospect at that age.

Frk has also been effective at the international level, putting up a point per game in the U18 tournament during the two years he played for the team. Martin was able to make the Czech Republic's World Junior Championship team despite turning 18 just 2 months prior. Not only was he effective, but he was the leading scoring forward for his country.

Martin has great size as he is over 6'0" and by now is likely over 200lbs. If this is true, it would not be a surprising fact, as Martin can play a physical style of game, and really doesn't look like a traditional European born player at all. He works hard along the boards, and can win battles. He uses his size effectively when carrying the puck by protecting it effectively, is strong on his feet, and isn't easily knocked off the puck. Martin has good offensive attributes and has a good release on his shot.

Looking forward to next season, Martin will be in the race for the top pick in the 2012 NHL Entry Draft, and will be a key part of a young Halifax Mooseheads team.

Morgan Reilly

Defense – Moose Jaw Warriors (WHL)
Born Mar 9 1994 - Vancouver, BC
Height 6.00 - Weight 190 - Shoots L

Games	Goals	Assists	Points	PIMS	+/-
65	6	22	28	21	-15

Morgan Reilly was drafted 2nd overall by the Moose Jaw Warriors and spent his 16 year old season with the Notre Dame Hounds. He dominated the league, as he was the leader in defensive scoring. Morgan played regularly with fellow 2012 prospect Slater Koekkoek of the OHL's Peterborough Petes.

Morgan Reilly is a player who, at the end of the year you'd think he'd be impossible to miss. However it was tough getting a good viewing on him early on. He started out caught behind rising prospect Joel Edmundson, and New York Rangers 1st Round Pick Dylan McIlrath, among others, relegating him to the 3rd pairing.

However, Morgan was able to display his talents, and earn more ice time, and became featured on the power play. When given a chance, Reilly proved his two-way potential. Morgan has shown great ability to move the puck, particularly on the power play. He can also shoot the puck when given the opportunity. Defensively, Reilly is a work in progress, but has shown some bright spots, and can hit as well. By playoff time Morgan was a positive impact for the Moose Jaw Warriors who eventually fell to the eventual WHL Champion Kootenay Ice. He put up a point in every game except one in the series. The elimination proved to be a blessing in disguise, as Morgan's skills were able to be highlighted on the national stage. We were extremely impressed with Reilly's performance throughout the tournament, and was critical for Canada's success.

Going into the 2012 NHL Entry Draft, Reilly absolutely has Top 10 potential, and the future looks bright. He will again be caught on a deep blueline, but after proving himself, Morgan will get top power play time, and will only continue to get better.

Ryan Murray

LW - Everett Silvertips (WHL)
Born Sep 27 ,1993 - White City, SASK
Height 6.00 - Weight 185 - Shoots L

Games	Goals	Assists	Points	PIMS	+/-
70	6	40	46	45	+18

Ryan Murray was the 9th Overall selection for the Everett Silvertips in the 2008 WHL Bantam Draft. Ryan will need to wait another season to be selected in the NHL Entry Draft due to his late birthday. Murray had to wait until 2009-2010 to play a full WHL season, and he quickly showed off his potential. Murray finished 2nd in defenseman scoring, then played well in the playoffs. He progressed as expected this year, and was named an assistant captain despite being only 17 at the time. Murray benefitted from the Tips early playoff exit being named the captain of Team Canada's U18 team. He along with top prospect Ryan Murphy, lead the team in scoring despite both being defensemen. Ryan has great leadership ability, and offensive instincts including strong puck moving abilities. Despite having great offensive abilities, Ryan is very reliable in his own zone and should be a very high pick for the 2012 NHL Entry draft.

Matia Marcantuoni

Center – Kitchener Rangers (OHL)
Born Feb 22 1994 -Toronto, ONT
Height 6.00 - Weight 189 - Shoots R

Games	Goals	Assists	Points	PIMS	+/-
42	11	16	27	26	-7

Matia Marcantuoni entered the 2010 OHL Draft as one of the highly touted players. However, after some draft reporting worries, Matia fell to #18 and became a huge steal for the Kitchener Rangers. Matia was shuffled through the lines, playing different roles at different times based on the Rangers needs. Due to the depth in Kitchener it caused Matia to appear as a fairly inconsistent player, having good performances some games, and being invisible in others. Marcantuoni has outstanding skating abilities, and is extremely elusive. One can only hope his hands are able to catch up to his feet this season, as he handles the puck fairly well, but needs to get quicker. Marcantuoni can set up offense for himself and others equally well, and is very dangerous when given space, or on a breakaway. Marcantuoni should play a top six role for the Rangers this season, and will hopefully be able to overcome his ankle injury that took him out of the line-up for most of the second half of the season, and greatly limited his effectiveness in the playoffs.

Henrik Samuelsson

RW/C - USNTSP (USHL)
Born Feb 7 1994 - Scottsdale, AZ
Height 6.02 - Weight 195 – Shoots R

Games	Goals	Assists	Points	PIMS	+/-
27	4	7	11	78	+1

Samuelsson is a dual citizen of both Sweden and USA, thanks to his father, former NHL Defenseman Ulf Samuelsson. Henrik is the younger brother of Pittsburgh Penguins' draft pick Philip. Henrik didn't want to follow the defensive family trend and has played as a forward. Henrik has had an interesting journey. He currently plays for the U.S. National Development program. Like his father and his brother Henrik has a bit of a mean streak attached to his game. Like both he also has outstanding size to develop with. At 6'2" already and barely 17 years old, he has a great frame to build into. Despite his age, he was a very effective part for the USNTDP and is effective in both creating offense for himself and others. While Philip has chosen the NCAA route of Boston College. Henrik has taken an odd route for a North American developed player, he will join MODO's U20 team. This likely has something to do with his father taking on the head coaching job for the men's team.

Dominik Volek

RW/C– HC Sparta Praha (U18)
Born Jan 12 1994 - Praha, CZE
Height 6.00 - Weight 168 - Shoots L

Games	Goals	Assists	Points	PIMS	+/-
42	11	16	27	26	-7

Dominik Volek is a top prospect out of the Czech Republic. Caught behind the spotlight of Martin Frk among Czech prospects, Dominik is showing he has some great potential going forward. He possesses average size, but put up good points for Sparta Praha's U18 team, where he also joined the U20 program for a short period of time, putting up a point per game. Volek has solid offensive potential. He has good hands, and skates up and down the ice well Volek has shown the ability to shoot the puck effectively, and does a good job of finding the right place to put the puck when he releases it. Dominik will be a player to watch, and should get at least a good look for the 2012 World Junior Championships.

5

PLAYER RANKINGS

HP RANK	NHL CS	PLAYER	POS	TEAM	Page
1	1	Nugent-Hopkins, Ryan	Center	Red Deer	1
2	1	Larsson, Adam	Defenseman	Skelleftea	2
3	3	Huberdeau, Jonathan	Center	Saint John	3
4	2	Zibanejad, Mika	Center	Djurgarden	4
5	6	Couturier, Sean	Center	Drummondville	5
6	2	Landeskog, Gabriel	Left Wing	Kitchener	6
7	9	Murphy, Ryan	Defenseman	Kitchener	7
8	5	Beaulieu, Nathan	Defenseman	Saint John	8
9	8	Strome, Ryan	Center	Niagara	9
10	14	McNeill, Mark	Center	Prince Albert	10
11	17	Rattie, Ty	Right Wing	Portland	11
12	18	Jenner, Boone	Center	Oshawa	12
13	7	Baertschi, Sven	Left Wing	Portland	13
14	24	Mayfield, Scott	Defenseman	Youngstown	14
15	6	Klefbom, Oscar	Defenseman	Farjestad	15
16	13	Oleksiak, Jamieson	Defenseman	Northeastern	16
17	12	Morrow, Joseph	Defenseman	Portland	17
18	10	Siemens, Duncan	Defenseman	Saskatoon	18
19	53	Percy, Stuart	Defenseman	Mississauga	19
20	3	Brodin, Jonas	Defenseman	Farjestad	20
21	4	Hamilton, Dougie	Defenseman	Niagara	21
22	4	Armia, Joel	Right Wing	Assat	21
23	28	Puempel, Matthew	Left Wing	Peterborough	22
24	16	Scheifele, Mark	Center	Barrie	24
25	36	Ritchie, Brett	Right Wing	Sarnia	25
26	22	Biggs, Tyler	Right Wing	USA U-18	26
27	19	Saad, Brandon	Left Wing	Saginaw	27
28	54	Sproul, Ryan	Defenseman	Sault Ste. Marie	28
29	20	Jurco, Tomas	Right Wing	Saint John	29
30	11	Namestnikov, Vladislav	Center	London	30
31	5	Jaskin, Dmitri	Right Wing	Slavia	31
32	21	Jensen, Nicklas	LW/RW	Oshawa	32
33	71	Cousins, Nick	Center	Sault Ste. Marie	33
34	37	Catenacci, Daniel	Center	Sault Ste. Marie	34
35	23	Miller, Jonathan	Center	USA U-18	35
36	35	Noesen, Stefan	Right Wing	Plymouth	36
37	15	Phillips, Zack	Center	Saint John	37
38	1	Gibson, John	Goalie	USA U-18	38
39	32	Grimaldi, Rocco	Center	USA U-18	39
40	43	Nieto, Matthew	Left Wing	Boston U	40
41	2	Gibson, Christopher	Goalie	Chicoutimi	41
42	1	Perhonen, Samu	Goalie	JYP JR.	42
43	11	Hofmann, Gregory	Center	Ambri	43
44	46	Lessio, Lucas	Left Wing	Oshawa	44
45	59	St. Croix, Michael	Center	Edmonton	45

HP RANK	NHL CS	PLAYER	POS	TEAM	Page
46	12	Rask, Victor	Center	Leksand	46
47	60	Ouellet, Xavier	Defenseman	Montreal	47
48	29	Khokhlachev, Alexander	LW/Center	Windsor	48
49	25	Murphy, Connor	Defenseman	USA U-18	49
50	34	Lucia, Mario	Left Wing	Wayzata	50
51	30	Rakell, Rickard	Right Wing	Plymouth	51
52	31	Ambroz, Seth	Right Wing	Omaha	52
53	33	Edmundson, Joel	Defenseman	Moose Jaw	53
54	61	Jacobs, Colin	Center	Seattle	54
55	63	Cramarossa, Joseph	Center	Mississauga	55
56		Kichton, Brenden	Defenseman	Spokane	56
57	40	Wotherspoon, Tyler	Defenseman	Portland	57
58	38	Musil, David	Defenseman	Vancouver	58
59	3	Binnington, Jordan	Goalie	Owen Sound	59
60	13	Honzik, David	Goalie	Victoriaville	60
61		Pageau, Jean-Gabriel	Center	Gatineau	102
62	42	Shaw, Logan	Right Wing	Cape Breton	79
63	17	Kucherov, Nikita	Wing	CSKA 2	110
64	50	Kuraly, Sean	Center	Indiana	113
65	56	Shore, Nicholas	Center	U. of Denver	115
66	58	Lowry, Adam	Left Wing	Swift Current	115
67	66	Ewanyk, Travis	Left Wing	Edmonton	116
68	83	Mersch, Michael	Left Wing	U. of Wisconsin	85
69	26	Prince, Shane	Center	Ottawa	94
70	72	Quine, Alan	Center	Peterborough	72
71	98	Harrington, Scott	Defenseman	London	64
72	45	Clendening, Adam	Defenseman	Boston U	112
73	41	Trocheck, Vincent	Center	Saginaw	67
74	49	Noebels, Marcel	Left Wing	Seattle	97
75		Leivo, Josh	Left Wing	Sudbury	124
76	113	Boucher, Reid	Center	USA U-18	132
77	8	Nermark, Joachim	Center	Linkoping Jr.	71
78	70	Larraza, Zac	Left Wing	USA U-18	119
79	57	Scarlett, Reece	Defenseman	Swift Current	108
80	27	Danault, Phillip	Left Wing	Victoriaville	62
81	39	Bell, Myles	Defenseman	Regina	76
82	73	Rieder, Tobias	Center	Kitchener	61
83	67	Racine, Jonathan	Defenseman	Shawinigan	100
84	69	Yuen, Zachary	Defenseman	Tri-City	135
85	55	Russo, Robbie	Defenseman	USA U-18	114
86	51	Labate, Joseph	Center	Holy Angels	114
87	14	Boyce, Jeremy	Left Wing	Timra	149
88	68	Lockhart, Luke	Right Wing	Seattle	99
89	74	Hudon, Philippe	RiW/Center	Choate-Rosemary	109
90	79	Meurs, Garrett	Center	Plymouth	86

HP RANK	NHL CS	PLAYER	POS	TEAM	Page
91	65	Archambault, Olivier	Left Wing	Val d'Or	75
92	44	Oke, Scott	Left Wing	Saint John	111
93	85	Pedan, Andrei	Defenseman	Guelph	88
94	8	Mahalak, Matt	Goalie	Plymouth	128
95	12	Williams, Jay	Goalie	Waterloo	133
96	135	Hietkamp, Luke	Right Wing	Peterborough	81
97	47	Tesink, Ryan	Center	Saint John	112
98		Zlobin, Anton	Left Wing	Shawinigan	118
99	10	Bengtsson, Rasmus	Defenseman	Rogle	146
100	199	Beaupre, Gabriel	Defenseman	Val d'Or	117
101	62	Le Sieur, Maximilien	Right Wing	Shawinigan	116
102	80	Reid, Adam	Left Wing	USA U-18	122
103	48	Welinski, Andy	Defenseman	Green Bay	130
104	179	Bell, Zach	Defenseman	Brampton	66
105	64	Brassard, Austen	Right Wing	Belleville	90
106	78	Camara, Anthony	Left Wing	Saginaw	69
107	101	Kessy, Kale	Left Wing	Medicine Hat	80
108	21	Karlsson, William	Center	Vasteras Jr.	145
109	111	Wittchow, Edward	Defenseman	Burnsville	82
110	18	Arzamastsev, Zakhar	Defenseman	Novokuznetsk	146
111	4	McNeely, Matt	Goalie	USA U-18	143
112	88	Lowe, Keegan	Defenseman	Edmonton	139
113	71	Blomqvist, Albin	Defenseman	Linkoping Jr.	149
114	121	Demelo, Dylan	Defenseman	Mississauga	93
115	104	Serville, Brennan	Defenseman	Stouffville	120
116	76	Koudys, Patrick	Defenseman	Rensselaer	136
117		Lieuwen, Nathan	Goalie	Kootenay	149
118		Heard, Mitchel	Center	Plymouth	87
119	84	Fritsch, Andrew	Right Wing	Owen Sound	63
120	125	McColgan, Shane	Right Wing	Kelowna	78
121	20	Arvidsson, Viktor	Left Wing	Skelleftea Jr.	145
122	90	Fogarty, Steven	Center	Edina High	140
123	130	Veilleux, Yannick	Left Wing	Shawinigan	103
124	103	Benson, Brent	Center	Saskatoon	77
125	106	Leblanc, Jean-Francois	Center	Val d'Or	107
126	148	Miller, Colin	Defenseman	Sault Ste. Marie	84
127	7	Salomaki, Miikka	Right Wing	Karpat	136
128	114	Pereira, Mike	Left Wing	U. Mass.	137
129	129	Andrews, Brent	Left Wing	Halifax	113
130	19	Houser, Michael	Goalie	London	133
131	9	Granlund, Markus	Center	HIFK JR.	141
132	32	Nesterov, Nikita	Defenseman	Chelyabinsk 2	143
133	86	Paliotta, Michael	Defenseman	USA U-18	129
134	81	Wuthrich, Austin	Right Wing	USA U-18	129
135	93	Everson, Max	Defenseman	Edina High	122

HP RANK	NHL CS	PLAYER	POS	TEAM	Page
136	202	Trojanovic, Steven	Defenseman	Peterborough	105
137	133	Elliot, Mitch	Left Wing	Seattle	119
138	146	Thomson, Ben	Left Wing	Kitchener	104
139	75	Sullivan, Colin	Defenseman	Avon Old Farms	139
140		Graves, Josh	Left Wing	Oshawa	106
141	105	Pietila, Blake	Left Wing	USA U-18	131
142	14	Ruby, Jordan	Goalie	Wellington	131
143		Sergeev, Artem	Defenseman	Val d'Or	118
144	152	Ferlin, Brian	Right Wing	Indiana	129
145	11	Machovsky, Matej	Goalie	Brampton	134
146	131	Hansen, Tyler	Defenseman	Kamloops	147
147	123	Franko, Zachery	Left Wing	Kelowna	111
148	96	Smith, Colin	Center	Kamloops	136
149	118	Duininck, Craig	Defenseman	Windsor	144
150	100	Straight, Destry	Center	Coquitlam	144
151	91	Grist, Sam	Defenseman	Tri-City	142
152	102	Ruopp, Harrison	Defenseman	Prince Albert	144
153	192	Sandlak, Carter	Left Wing	Belleville	89
154	134	Harstad, Aaron	Defenseman	Green Bay	134
155		Findlay, Brett	Left Wing	Sault Ste. Marie	70
156	117	Donnelly, Dillon	Defenseman	Shawinigan	141
157	155	Corrado, Frank	Defenseman	Sudbury	121
158		Mitchell, Zack	Right Wing	Guelph	110
159	120	Graovac, Tyler	Center	Ottawa	126
160		Basso, Alex	Defenseman	Belleville	74
161	33	Bjorklund, Gustav	Center	Vasteras Jr.	138
162	82	Curtis, Michael	Left Wing	Belleville	121
163		Maillet, Philippe	Center	Victoriaville	95
164	159	Windle, Samuel	Defenseman	Des Moines	137
165		Lepkowski, Alex	Defenseman	Barrie	68
166	156	Henley, Samuel	Left Wing	Lewiston	139
167	158	Griffith, Seth	Center	London	92
168		Hall, Zach	Center	Barrie	148
169	138	Dietz, Darren	Defenseman	Saskatoon	
170	132	Saar, Zach	Right Wing	Chicago	134
171	15	Galansky, Tadeas	Goalie	Saginaw	147
172	94	Kelly, Aidan	Center	Saint John	142
173		Di Giuseppe Phil	Left Wing	Villanova	120
174	143	Carlson, Dan	Left Wing	USA U-18	132
175		Shaw, Andrew	Center	Owen Sound	
176	34	Shalunov, Maxim	Right Wing	Chelyabinsk 2	147
177	164	Willick, Dylan	Right Wing	Kamloops	148
178	6	Morrison, Michael	Goalie	Kitchener	91
179	92	Bourret, Gabriel	Defenseman	Saint John	138
180	157	Simpson, Dillon	Defenseman	North Dakota	148

HP RANK	NHL CS	PLAYER	POS	TEAM	Page
181		Francisco, Brandon	Left Wing	Sarnia	65
182	122	Bardaro, Anthony	Center	Spokane	
183		Janes, Steven	Right Wing	Ottawa	126
184	168	Bunnett, Brian	Center	Wellington	128
185	137	Cloutier, Guillaume	Defenseman	Chicoutimi	96
186	166	Forsberg, Jesse	Defenseman	Prince George	123
187		Steeves, Robert	Goalie	Acadie Bathurst	138
188	77	St. Clair, Colten	Center	Fargo	128
189	7	Brossoit, Laurent	Goalie	Edmonton	
190		Drost, Colby	Goalie	New England	145
191		Moffatt, Mike	Defenseman	London	73
192	21	Lagace, Maxime	Goalie	PEI	135
193	52	Reilly, Mike	Defenseman	Shattuck-	140
194	29	Palazzese, Frank	Goalie	Kingston	124
195	13	Friberg, Max	Left Wing	Skovde	135
196	139	Broll, David	Left Wing	Sault Ste. Marie	83
197	107	O'Gara, Rob	Defenseman	Milton Academy	
198		Currie Josh	Left Wing	PEI	117
199	183	Noreau, Samuel	Defenseman	Baie Comeau	141
200	108	Didier, Josiah	Defenseman	Cedar Rapids	131
201	26	Teichmann, Tyson	Goalie	Belleville	127
202	112	Wyszomirski, Craig	Defenseman	The Gunnery	
203	147	Woods, Brendan	Left Wing	Muskegon	130
204		Mathers, Derek	Right Wing	Peterborough	
205	9	Liston, Liam	Goalie	Brandon	98
206	109	Miller, Stephen	Left Wing	Nobles	
207		Rose, Brayden	Defenseman	Owen Sound	125
208	119	Haar, Garrett	Defenseman	Fargo	133
209	99	Wruck, Dylan	Center	Edmonton	142
210		Brace, Cameron	Right Wing	Owen Sound	126
-	126	King, Michael	Defenseman	Westside	
-	17	Sparks, Garret	Goalie	Guelph	
-	149	Vance, Troy	Defenseman	Victoriaville	
-	116	Goodrow, Barclay	Left Wing	Brampton	123
-	110	Gill, Sahir	Center	Boston U	
-		Smoskowitz, Dylan	Center	Barrie	125
-	127	Morris, Kevin	Left Wing	Salisbury	
-		Austin, Brady	Defenseman	Erie	122
-	201	Leonard, Curtis	Defenseman	Wellington	130
-		Cason Hohmann	Center	Cedar Rapids	101
-	161	McCormick, Max	Left Wing	Sioux City	137
-	128	Fiddler, Todd	Left Wing	Prince Albert	
-	89	Sefton, Justin	Defenseman	Sudbury	123
-	140	Suellentrop, Colin	Defenseman	Oshawa	
-	24	Sundstrom, Johan	Center	Frolunda	146

HP RANK	NHL CS	PLAYER	POS	TEAM	Page
-	124	Cameron, Jason	Center	Saint John	
-	208	McNaughton, Cody	Right Wing	Guelph	109
-	115	Czarnik, Austin	Center	Green Bay	132
-	87	Cutting, Keevin	Defenseman	Owen Sound	140
-		MacLeod, Matt	Left Wing	Brampton	121
-		Malysa, Nick	Defenceman	Plymouth	143
-		Foglia, Nick	RW,Center	Ottawa	127
-		Beranek,Petr	Right Wing	Barrie	124
-		Auld, Jordan	Defenseman	Brampton	125
-		Evan Rodrigues		Georgetown	

KEY

HP Rank – HockeyProspect.com Ranking
NHL CS – NHL Central Scouting Ranking

Note: The NHL Central Scouting Rankings were obtained from their final rankings. The number shown is the players ranking within either North American or Europe.

Photo Credits

We want to thank Terry Wilson and Aaron Bell from OHL IMAGES for the use of their OHL, WHL and QMJHL player photos.

We also want to thank all the other photographers who allowed us to show off their work.

Cover photos also from www.chlimages.ca

David Arnold - USHL http://dga17.smugmug.com/

WHL, OHL, QMJHL for their photos

The USHL for photos from USHL Images

Marc Grandmaison QMJHL Photos
www.marcgrandmaison.com

Joe Versikaitis http://www.versikaitis.com

David Connell Photography

Adam Crane MN hockey hub

Elite Prospects

Kyle Scholzen/Seattle Thunderbirds

Kevin Prahl - Oscar Klefbom

Cory Kerr – Moose Jaw Warriors

Timothy Kane Photography

HockeyProspect.com

Founder

 Mark Edwards

Scouts

Mark Edwards
Ron Berman
Rob Basso
Dave Toledano
Bruno Simard
Ryan Yessie
Simon Larouche
Jason Hills
Justin Schreiber
Risto Ahonen

And a few guys who prefer to remain nameless…

Website and Media

Steve Fitzsimmons
Cameron Rudolph
Michelle Sturino
Alex Linsky

HockeyProspect.com also takes advantage of a huge network of fantastic hockey people we use worldwide. There are instances where we need extra input or information on a player. We are able to shrink the globe and call on these contacts.

We always remember the late Jim Koleff for helping us build a few of these relationships.

2011-2012

After the NHL Draft in June we will be working through July making some changes to our website. The changes will be made to both the front end and in the 'nuts and bolts' of the website in the back end. Our goal is to improve the way we provide information to both INSIDERS and the casual fan seeking information on hockey prospects.

Stay up to date with the most recent information leading up to the NHL Draft.

Visit HockeyProspect.com for all your prospect news.

HockeyProspect.com
contact@hockeyprospect.com

1.877.473.7238

OAKVILLE ONTARIO
CANADA

www.ingramcontent.com/pod-product-compliance
Lightning Source LLC
LaVergne TN
LVHW081352060426
835510LV00013B/1790